Girl of the Wild

Girl of the Wild

Misadventures in the African Bush

By Rosie Miles

The right of Rosie Miles to be identified as author of this work has been asserted by the author in accordance with the Copyright, Designs and Patents Act 1988

Copyright © 2021 Rosie Miles

All rights reserved. No part of this publication may be reproduced, distributed, or transmitted in any form or by any means, including photocopying, recording, or other electronic or mechanical methods, without the prior written permission of the publisher, except in the case of brief quotations embodied in critical reviews and certain other non-commercial uses permitted by copyright law. For permission requests, write to the publisher at the address below.

Published by Just Jhoom! Ltd
PO Box 142
Cranleigh, Surrey
GU6 8ZX
www.justjhoom.co.uk

Cover Design: Stuart Kinlough
Author Photo: Victoria Cooke

ISBN:

This book is dedicated to all Girls of the Wild

Table of Contents

Foreword		9
Introduction		13
Chapter 1	P.S. I Want to be a Safari Guide	18
Chapter 2	The New Normal	38
Chapter 3	Learning Lessons the Hard Way	54
Chapter 4	~~Fake It~~ Practice 'Til You Make It	77
Chapter 5	Misadventures of the Venomous Kind	100
Chapter 6	Misadventures of the Terrorist Kind	120
Chapter 7	Misadventures of the Meat-Eating Kind	133
Chapter 8	Misadventures of the Giant, Grey Kind	158
Chapter 9	Misadventures of the Horny Kind	173
Chapter 10	It's Not the Wildlife You Need to Worry About	189
Chapter 11	Going Home	216
Epilogue		236
Quote Credits		242
Photo and Design Credits		244
Acknowledgements		245
A Note from the Author		248
About the Author		249

"Her mother told her
She could grow up to be
Anything she wanted to be.
So she grew up to become
The strongest of the strong
The strangest of the strange
The wildest of the wild
The wolf leading the wolves."

- Nikita Gill[1]

Foreword

I was fortunate to have been born and brought up in Kenya – a beautiful country with an abundance of wildlife. As children, my father would pile us into his Nissan Sunny at weekends and drive off to Amboseli at the foot of Mount Kilimanjaro to see elephants or to the plains of Maasai Mara to see the majestic lions. If time was short, then a trip to the Nairobi National Park was always on the cards – especially on a Sunday morning when we would spend three to four hours looking for rhinos, lions and cheetah. I always liken us going on safari to people in England going to the cinema. Going on safari was something that was normal for us – in fact I can't even remember my first safari. Yes – it was a beautiful, privileged childhood – and I am so grateful for it.

You may think that one would get bored of this. After all, if you have seen one elephant, then you've seen them all. Or if you've seen a lion, then surely that's it. How exciting can they be? Very as it happens. No matter how many times I see a lion or an elephant or a leopard I am always in awe of these beautiful creatures. But, it isn't just the big animals that take your breath away. To see a male ostrich doing his mating dance, or two male impala fighting or a family of warthogs running across the road, tails up in the air – these are sights that really stay with you.

My sister Shivani was so influenced by these childhood experiences that she went on to become a lion conservationist and set up her own hugely successful conservation project Ewaso Lions in Samburu, northern Kenya.

And it is because of her that I met Rosie.

In February 2020, I was working for my sister at a Pathways Conservation Conference in Limuru, Kenya which Rosie happened to be attending. Serendipity meant that we shared a car back to Nairobi at the end of the conference and we chatted all the way. One of the advantages of social media is the ease with which we were able to keep in touch – and a friendship was born.

When Rosie said she wanted to be on my new Pen to Published course and write a memoir about her work in Africa, I was absolutely delighted. And when you read this book, you will see why.

Rosie has written a book about her wildlife experiences to rival any other book in this genre. Her adventures, or misadventures, as she trained as a safari guide and then worked in various roles in southern Africa will keep you riveted. I laughed out aloud as she described the antics of the monkeys in her tent, held my breath as she recounted catching a black mamba, and teared-up as she bade farewell to her beloved elephants. I couldn't put this book down – it is a real page turner. And, every page reminded me of just how beautiful, wild, dangerous and enchanting Africa is. And, it is people like Rosie who work hard to protect this precious resource of ours – the wildlife of Africa.

I know that you, like me, will be transported to the places and situations that Rosie describes in this book – as she evokes the sights, sounds and smells of the wild. And, just like Rosie, you too will feel like a "Girl of the Wild", even if it is just for a few hours.

Shalini Bhalla-Lucas
Nairobi, 2021
@justjhoom
www.justjhoom.co.uk

Introduction

I haven't always been wild.

My unruly hair aside – which earned me the nickname "The Curly Headed Monster" as a child - the first 29 years of my life were pretty tame.

Growing up in rural England, I always loved the outdoors, but I wasn't the kind of kid that played in the dirt and caught bugs. I had aspirations of being a vet and volunteered at the local clinic, but I never brought injured wildlife home to rehabilitate. I loved animals and had a curiosity about the natural world, but I didn't spend hours losing myself in the wilderness. My interactions with wildlife were limited to an unhealthy obsession with nature documentaries on TV. A physical connection with wildlife wasn't a dominant feature of my life growing up.

But Africa was.

I was lucky enough to grow up with my grandparents in the same house. Every day after school, I would have a cup of tea and freshly baked cake with my granny in her sitting room. The room was dark and cluttered with antique furniture, just like many grandparents' houses. The difference in my granny's though, was that it was decorated with paintings and souvenirs from Africa. During those afternoon teas, she would regale me with stories of her childhood spent travelling from port to port around the continent of Africa as her family sailed back and forth between Mauritius, where she grew up, and the family home in the Outer Hebrides of Scotland.

I was captivated by her stories. As she talked, I would potter around the room looking at the black and white, geometric patterns in the paintings of gemsbok antelope. I loved to run my fingers over the cool, black, stone elephant carving that was the size of a small dog. The fairy tales I was told as a kid weren't from any book, they were the real-life adventures my granny had as a child in Africa.

It wasn't just my granny's influence though. My parents' sitting room had its own African adornments, including more paintings of gemsbok - it is little wonder these have always been my favourite antelope. The collection had been started by my dad after travelling around Southern Africa at 18 years old, but the number of items expanded year on year as various members of the family travelled back and forth to the continent. Stories and images of Africa were a constant in our house, and so, for me there was never any doubt that I, too, would set foot on the continent at some point in my life.

What I didn't expect, however, was the hold the wildlife would have over me once I did.

I spent the better part of high school planning to train as a vet. However, in my final year, I inexplicably changed my mind and applied to study astrophysics at university instead. So, when I embarked on my first trip to Africa, before starting my degree, wildlife wasn't actually at the forefront of my mind. Coming from a family of teachers, doctors and social scientists, it was the people and culture that I was primarily interested in. However, once immersed in the savannah and in the presence of the incredible animals I had been watching fixatedly on TV, I had an overwhelming sense that this was where I was meant to be. There was a feeling deep in my gut that this was my natural habitat - that being in the wild, surrounded by animals, was my calling. A small seed was planted inside my heart.

But for the next decade, that seed lay dormant.

On returning to the UK to start university, I suppressed the call of the wild, and settled into a normal, stable life. I forced myself to forget how at home I felt in the African bush because that couldn't be my reality. Living a life in the wild could only ever be a dream, especially for a not-very-wild girl from England. Or so I thought.

But one day, ten years later, something happened that changed my mind.

I have always had a propensity for making unexpected decisions, causing great confusion and anxiety for my parents. In this case, however, the idea to do the unexpected wasn't my own. An email from my mum stirred up those feelings again and caused that dormant seed to sprout, setting me on a path of no return to a life in the wild. I will never know what possessed my mum to suggest her youngest child pack up her life to go live in the wilds of Africa. Or whether she now regrets sending that email, given the content of the text communications she has endured ever since.

At 29 years old, having only experienced one short safari ten years earlier, I gave up the security of an ordinary life and embarked on an adventure of a lifetime. In this book, I share just a few of the comical, scary, and difficult misadventures that took me from an ordinary English girl to a not-so-ordinary *Girl of the Wild*.

> *"She had a gypsy soul and a warrior spirit.*
> *She made no apologies for her wild heart.*
> *She left normal and regular to*
> *explore the outskirts*
> *of magical and extraordinary."*
>
> *- Michelle Rose Gilman*[2]

Chapter 1

P.S. I Want to be a Safari Guide

```
TEXT RECEIVED [15:01:2010, 21:43:05]
ROSIE: Hi Mum. Arrived safe and sound. There
is a spitting cobra in the shower - apparently
it lives there...
```

The UK was experiencing the coldest winter since the 1970s. Temperatures in North Yorkshire had dipped as low as -15°C. With snow covering the ground, we hadn't been able to get the Land Rover up to the house for weeks. The track was treacherously icy and snowdrifts, more than a metre deep in some places, blocked the farm gates. Yet, I was packing a suitcase with shorts, t-shirts and sun cream.

In less than 24 hours, I would land in Johannesburg, and then, on to the African bush. I was starting my training as a safari guide.

I first set foot on the African continent ten years earlier, straight after finishing school. While "gap years" were still unusual in those days, they had long been a tradition in my family and it never crossed my mind that I wouldn't take one.

It was on this gap year in East Africa that I went on my first safari. During my teenage years, while my friends were watching MTV, I sat glued to the Animal Planet channel. I was completely bewitched by the African savannah and by big cats in particular. I was transfixed by their golden colours blending perfectly with those of the vast, open grasslands. Their lithe bodies and slinking movements coupled with their strength and brutality, it mesmerized me. I was a big cat junkie. I knew far more about the animals of the savannah than the creatures found in my own backyard in the UK. Seeing them in the flesh for the first time was electrifying and it had a profound impact on my life from that point forwards.

The safari took us through the stunning Samburu National Reserve, an arid grassland area in the north of Kenya. At the time, Kenya was in the grip of an intense drought. Dusty and overpoweringly hot, Samburu was a parched landscape. As we drove around in our huge, open-sided, overland truck, dust-devils whipped up and mirages shimmered on the horizon. The drought was both an ecological and humanitarian disaster, but in my ignorant, young mind, this was the picture of Africa I had been dreaming of for so many years.

Every so often a more distinct dust cloud would appear in the distance. As one of these clouds moved closer to the vehicle, I realised it was being stirred up by the hundred plodding feet of a family of elephants. In single file, they silently marched passed without even a cursory glance in our direction. In my subsequent wisdom, I understand why. During a drought year, there's no time for pleasantries or curiosity. There is only urgency to find enough water to satiate the family, each elephant needing around 150 litres a day, or else the babies in the herd won't survive. The Ewaso Nyiro river, which cuts through the Samburu National Reserve and is normally a lifeblood for the wildlife, had shrunk to a few muddy pools. The matriarch leading the family was on a mission to find one of the last remaining pools big enough to slake their thirst.

After the herd passed by, I spotted something appearing through the settling dust. Two enormous black-maned lions - regal and relaxed - trailing behind the elephants. For predators, droughts can be a blessing rather than a disaster. Prey animals, weakened by a lack of food and water, make for easy pickings. In many cases, lions don't even have to get their hands dirty with the messy, and often dangerous, business of killing prey. Scavenging on those fallen as a result of starvation is like having a supermarket ready-meal. These lions, patiently following the elephants, were sinisterly waiting for the weakest to fall onto their plates.

Camera in hand, I leant over the side of the truck to get level with the lions, hoping for a dramatic photo opportunity. Someone behind me shouted, "Look! Lions!" and without warning, I was pinned down by the weight of three people clambering over the top of me to get a better view.

Unable to move, I lay there as the two lions strutted along the side of the vehicle, using the shade it created as a brief respite from the scorching sun. I watched the giant, fuzzy heads move seemingly in slow motion, one after the other, beneath me. They were less than a metre away from my face. I felt the heat radiating off their bodies. I heard the deep rasping of their breath and smelled the musty odour of their fur. I breathed it all in. If I had been able to move my arms, I might have been tempted to reach out and touch them. It was a good job I couldn't. While I was completely still, they paid me no more attention than the elephants had. If I had been foolish enough to move, this story could have had a very different ending.

The lions continued on, disappearing into the haze of the dust following the elephants. "Did you get some good photos, Rosie?", one of the others asked, the weight on top of me lifting as they returned to their seats.

"Uh no," I replied, "You idiots nearly got my face eaten off! Did you not realise you had me pinned over the side?" I rolled my eyes at them to show my frustration, but inside, my heart was popping like a firecracker from the exhilaration.

That afternoon, I wrote a letter to my mum.

> *Hi mum*
>
> *These are all the foods I am missing, please can you make sure we have them in the house when I get back:*
> *Bacon*
> *Cheese and Onion Walkers*
> *Marmite*

Sausage rolls
Cadbury Mini Eggs.... [the list went on for a full page]

Lots of love,
Rosie

P.S. I want to be a safari guide.

When I got home a few months later, the pantry was dutifully stocked as requested. However, the ridiculous notion to become a safari guide, so flippantly added as a postscript, was noticeably absent from conversation.

Shortly after my return, a series came on TV following a group of wannabe safari guides from all over the world. Teachers, lawyers, plumbers and the like, all with no previous experience, joined a residential programme in South Africa to train as guides. My mum and I watched the series together religiously. I was vicariously living every moment, painfully jealous of their experience and thinking *I could do that too. I stared a lion in the face. And I know everything about African wildlife because I have watched every nature documentary there is.*

September rolled round though, and my sense of responsibility took over. With the notion of becoming a safari guide safely packed away as a pipe dream, I obediently headed off to university. The years ticked by. My undergraduate degree turned into a postgraduate degree and involved a relocation to New Zealand - not a country known for its big cats or any other large mammals for that matter.

After graduation, I walked into a respectable job in local government. Over the next few years I was quickly promoted up the ranks. My life was mapped out in front of me and I was happy. I had job satisfaction, an amazing circle of friends and a work-life balance that was second to none. What more could I want?

Then one morning, over breakfast, I was surfing the estate agent website looking for a nice cottage to buy in the suburbs, when *ping*, an email notification popped up on the screen. It was from my mum.

All it said was, "Didn't you always want to do this?"

Underneath this solitary sentence was a link to a website for "Safari School". My heart skipped a beat. She had found the website for the same training programme that was featured on the TV programme so many years earlier. I clicked on the link and opened Pandora's box. The emotions I had felt all those years earlier in the presence of those elephants and lions in Samburu came flooding back. There were no questions in my mind, no hesitation. My ordinary life was about to change course.

A few months later, having applied for a year-long sabbatical from work, I packed up my house and prepared for my new, wild life. The plan was to do a 12-month training programme, just to get it out of my system. Then, I would come back to the real world and get on with my life. At least, this was what I said publicly. Deep down, I knew returning to a normal life was unlikely. I would find a home in the African bush.

Ten years on from my first safari, that throw-away postscript in the letter to my mum was about to become a reality. I was going to become a qualified safari guide under the Field Guides Association of Southern Africa (FGASA).

Bags packed, we sledged down the hill to the car. At the airport, I stripped off my down jacket and moonboots, opting for attire more suitable to the Southern African summer.

Handing the clothing to my mum, she said, "Aren't you scared?"

I shrugged, "No, why would I be?"

It was a genuine response. I didn't feel even a hint of anxiety about the adventure that lay before me. I hugged both my parents goodbye and skipped excitedly to the departure lounge.

The arrivals hall at Johannesburg airport bustled with activity, but it wasn't hard to spot my 11 classmates with whom I would spend the next six months. Wide-brimmed khaki hats and sturdy walking boots gave us all away. Once assembled, we were whisked away in a minibus out of the city and towards the wilderness.

The highway was flanked on both sides by mile after mile of open grassland interspersed with generic farmland crops. There was little wildlife to be seen. My excitement faltered momentarily looking out at this uninspiring landscape. I started to wonder if South Africa was going to be as exhilarating as Kenya. Or whether in fact my memories from ten years earlier had become rose-tinted with time.

However, after a few hours the highway gave way to smaller, winding roads. The grasslands morphed into verdant mountains looming on all sides. Without warning everything went dark. We had entered a tunnel that passed straight through the mountains. Emerging from the other side, the sight that lay before me took my breath away. In front of us, the mountains stopped abruptly, giving way to vast plains more than 1,000 metres below. It felt like you could see to the end of the earth. Even at that distance I could make out the bare criss-cross of game trails through the trees, cut by thousands of animal feet on their daily march to favoured waterholes. I was back in the "Africa" I remembered.

As we descended to the plains below, our driver explained that we had just crossed the famous Drakensberg mountain range that runs the length of South Africa. Since our arrival in Johannesburg we had been driving on a high plateau around 1,500m above sea level. On the eastern side of the Drakensberg, the mountains end sharply, forming an escarpment and giving the range a characteristic wedge-shape appearance. 'Drakensberg' comes from the Afrikaans word *Drakensberge*, meaning 'Dragon's Mountains'. To many, the wedges of the escarpment resemble the spikes running down the back of a dragon. Everything east of the escarpment is known as the lowveld, pronounced *low-felt*, literally 'low field'. The lowveld is the land of the safaris, home to the world-famous Kruger National Park, and where we were going to be doing our training.

Now, driving along the plains at the bottom, I could see the road was lined on both sides by 2.4-metre-high electric fences. Every few metres, there was a yellow hazard sign stating "Danger" with an electric bolt symbol. In between the danger signs, were red and white triangular warning signs with silhouettes of animals, similar to the UK signs warning of deer crossing. In this instance though, the silhouettes were of elephant and lion. It made me giggle. *What kind of place has to warn you of elephants and lions crossing?* I thought to myself.

The minibus came to a stop outside an elaborately turreted entrance gate into one of these fenced-off zones. Parked on either side, as if to welcome us, two open-topped, 11-seater Land Rover game-viewers sat idle. My heart buzzed again. My safari adventure was about to begin.

It was already dusk by the time we piled into the game-viewers, packed like sardines with our suitcases wedged between us. Our new drivers introduced themselves as our trainers. They would spend the next six months with us, teaching us everything we needed to know to be safari guides. Instantly, I could pick up their unique personalities. The head trainer was the quiet, serious one. Someone to be revered and respected. The second was the cool cat - supremely chilled and oozing confidence. The third was a joker with a grin that reached ear to ear. He had a glint in his eye that suggested he knew exactly what emotions were running through our heads at the moment. And that's because he did. He had completed the same course only a few years earlier. My truck was being driven by the Joker and the Cool Cat, which felt like a good combination.

We set off in a convoy, but at the first junction in the road the two vehicles separated. The Joker shouted back at us, "We don't want to eat their dust all the way home, so we'll go a different way."
The Cool Cat added, "It's about an hour-and-a-half's drive from here."

The wind, rushing past my ears in the open vehicle, carried the words away from me. I tapped on the shoulder of the girl sitting in front of me and asked, "Did they just say an hour-and-a-half?"

"Yes," she replied.

"Wow! It will be dark soon. A night drive on our first night."

I sat back, my grin now also stretching ear to ear. I could barely believe that only hours ago I had been sledging through the snow to get to the airport. Now, it was almost dark, and I was in only a t-shirt. Despite the exposure of the open vehicle, I felt comfortably enveloped in a warm, humid blanket.

For the first half an hour, my fellow passengers and I filled the air with excited whooping and giggles verging on hysteria. We must have sounded like a pack of hyena to anyone downwind. After a while, the mania abated and we lulled into silence as everyone stared intently into the darkness, trying to absorb as much of our new surroundings as possible.

Even above the noise of the truck and wind, I could hear the sounds of the night crescendo. I heard various types of frogs and insects, maybe even an owl or two. While I couldn't identify them yet, I was excited at the thought of learning what all these strange sounds were over the coming months. The headlights jumped from tree to tree, creating distorted shadows. On more than one occasion, I thought the unfamiliar shapes might have been a lion or a leopard. I reassured myself that the Cool Cat and the Joker would stop if there was something exciting to see. Perhaps, it was simply my eager eyes playing tricks on me.

A crackle came over the radio, but I couldn't hear what was being said. The Cool Cat picked up the mouthpiece and responded. We looked on expectantly. Casually, he turned in his seat to face us.

"That was base," he said. "They say there's a leopard outside the house calling. Do you want to go look for it or do you want to go straight to the house?"
Uh, stupid question?!

Once again, the truck erupted into hysterical whooping. It was decided, we would go look for the leopard.

We drove round and round, stopping and switching off the engine now and then to listen for the characteristic call of a leopard - the sound of sawing wood. We heard it twice. The first time was so close I felt the reverberations in my chest.

We waited.

The tension was palpable. Eight people silently wishing for the same thing - a leopard to step out of the bushes into our headlights. A few minutes later, when it called a second time, the leopard was now further away. In true leopard style, it had kept in the shadows and slunk away into the darkness. We were not to see the leopard that night, but hearing one that close, before even arriving at our destination, was a fantastic start to our course. We admitted defeat and headed for base.

The other truck was already at the house and the rest of the class was sitting outside on the porch waiting for our arrival. The Serious One introduced us to the camp staff and gave us a tour and safety briefing. In the darkness, it was impossible to get an impression of the surroundings, that would have to wait until morning. But inside, the house was a large, brightly lit, double-height barn. The main part of the house was an open-plan room that served as the kitchen, lounge and dining room. Off to the sides sat three dormitory-style bedrooms with a fourth on a mezzanine floor above. Much to my delight, I was allocated a small twin room with a quiet South African girl. I like to have a peaceful space to retreat to when I need to recharge my introvert batteries.

At the back of the house, across a small courtyard, was the bathroom block with a couple of showers and a toilet.

"Always use a torch when walking to the bathroom," the Serious One said. No further details or explanations were given.

The two trucks exchanged stories about the drive to base as we settled in and got to know each other. For dinner, we were served delicious coronation chicken. It is a real favourite of mine - I used to request it for my birthday every year. As a massive foodie, I decided this was a good sign.

I headed to my room to unpack. As a habitual nester, I have to unpack straight away and designate places for all my belongings. I like to feel at home from the outset. It helps me settle into a new place quickly and sleep more soundly. Once unpacked, I put up my mosquito net. I rarely sleep without one if I can help it. Not just to keep the mosquitoes out, I also prefer to sleep knowing that I won't be joined in the night by any other creatures either.

As I was standing on my bed tying up the net, I heard someone shouting expletives. I poked my head through my bedroom door just in time to see one of my fellow students come flying through the back door wearing nothing but a towel.

"There's an effing huge snake in the shower!"

The guy explained he had been in the shower when he felt something cold and smooth slither over his foot. When he looked down there was a metre-long pale grey snake that had nonchalantly joined him in the shower.

The Serious One came to see what the commotion was. He advised that it was a Mozambique spitting cobra. Apparently, she was a regular visitor to the showers, lured by the many frogs who were attracted by the moisture created from our daily washing activities.

"We will catch and relocate her, but she'll most likely be back again in a day or two. It's best to just keep an eye out for her and not go in if she's there."

The "use a torch" advice given earlier suddenly had context. While our formal lessons didn't start until morning, it seems bush life lessons happen on the fly here. Night one, lesson one - how to stay safe around snakes that live in the shower.

The Cool Cat arrived with a round bucket with a clip-on lid and a long tong-like contraption that resembled the sticks groundskeepers use to pick up litter back home. He was also wearing safety goggles and a headtorch. He disappeared into the shower block while the Serious One continued to lecture us on snakes, and more specifically this particular snake.

The lecture closed with a warning, "It's her babies you should be most concerned about. They are all over the garden and much more prone to spitting. Feisty little buggers," he said. "Luckily, at the moment, their range doesn't quite reach head height, so they won't get you in the eyes if you are standing upright. But I advise against bending down when you are walking around the rockery."

I decided I probably didn't need a shower tonight, nor did I need to spend much time in the rockery, ever.

As the Serious One finished up his talk, the Cool Cat emerged again with the bucket, its lid now tightly secured. Through the walls of the clear plastic I could see the unmistakable shadow of a snake crawling about. I felt a shiver run down my spine. It was thrilling but not in quite the same way the lion had been ten years earlier. I wasn't sure how I felt about sharing my bathroom with deadly snakes. I was going to have to sleep on that one.

The excitement over, I headed to bed. Eager for tomorrow when the lessons would really start. I got into bed and picked up my phone, *better just let mum know I have arrived safe and the excitement has already begun*, I thought.

> *"And then she learnt to be a little wild*
> *She had to be a little less afraid."*
> *- Nikki Rowe*[3]

Chapter 2

The New Normal

```
TEXT RECEIVED [04:02:2010, 07:30:20]
ROSIE: Hi Mum. A leopard walks into a bar... No,
this is not a joke...
```

The next morning, with the sun up, we took in our surroundings. The farmhouse was set in a large, manicured garden. My eyes were immediately drawn to a swimming pool sparkling in the sunlight. It looked so inviting and refreshing, as I stood there already sweating at 6 a.m., not yet adjusted to the new climate. Beyond the pool was a beach volleyball court. For the last few months, an evening game of volleyball had become my routine. So, I was pleased my new skills would not go to waste. I couldn't help but feel the garden looked more like a holiday camp than a place of learning. *This is my kind of setup*, I thought.

An electric fence enclosed the garden. Unlike the 2.4-metre-high ones we had seen on the drive in though, this was only a foot high. *That's not keeping lions and elephants out?* I mused. The Serious One confirmed the fence was only there to keep the warthogs from decimating the garden. He gave us a grave warning not to assume the fence provided any form of additional protection.

At the rear of the farmhouse lay a dry, sandy riverbed lined with dense riverine trees. *Perfect leopard habitat,* I noted, as the Serious One dished out another warning not to wander down into the riverbed. We were only to go there in the company of a trainer.

To the front, the house looked out over a bush airstrip, a bare patch of ground 100 metres wide and over a kilometre long. The Joker asked if anyone liked to play football. "We can play on the airstrip, so long as we check for lions first, and someone keeps watch."

Keep watch for lions, while we run around chasing a ball? I couldn't decide if he was joking or not. Turns out he wasn't. Football matches on the airstrip became a regular activity, when there weren't any lions about.

While I was still contemplating the idea of having lions as spectators to our football matches, there was a crackle over the radio from inside the house.

"Farmhouse, come in."

Heading back inside, the Serious One picked up the mouthpiece and responded, "Standing by."

"I've got those two cheetah brothers drinking at the pond at this end of the airstrip if your new students want to come have a look."

"Copy that. On our way."

And with that, we were instructed to pile into the two Land Rovers. This was part of the new normal - no matter what activity we were currently engaged in, we might have to drop it in the blink of an eye. You cannot schedule nature, you simply have to go with the flow. We also quickly learnt that a crackle over the radio usually meant something exciting was going to happen. From then on, the first sound of static always drew great anticipation.

We cruised along the airstrip. The impala and wildebeest that were grazing, parted as we drove through them, only to return again as soon as we passed. The Joker explained that antelope like to graze on the airstrip because it's open, making it harder for predators to ambush them. But I knew, from my many hours watching the Animal Planet documentaries, that cheetahs are not normally ambush hunters like leopards and lions. They prefer to hunt in open habitat where they can use their lightning speed to chase down prey. My mind wandered and my heartbeat quickened with expectation. *Are we about to see our first hunt?*

Arriving at the pond, however, it became clear that these cheetahs would not be hunting today. Their bellies were enormous. It looked like they had each swallowed a whole watermelon. The impala could relax, these cats were only interested in washing down their latest meal. They would probably spend the rest of the day sleeping off the feast in the shade of a tree.

A hunt was off the table, but the sighting did not disappoint. Cheetah have been my favourite animal for as long as I can remember. And, less than 12 hours after we arrived, I was sitting a few metres away from two of them. The brothers were crouched on their haunches, delicately lapping water from the pond. Their identical faces, each a mirror image of the other, were being reflected in the glassy water creating a kaleidoscope of cheetah faces.

Click, click, click.

Everyone's cameras were out. In the early morning light, the golden pelts of the cats glowed. Their amber eyes burned like hot liquid magma. Though they paid little attention to us, or the shutters of our cameras, they were not relaxed. A cheetah is rarely relaxed. Their heads constantly turning left and right, and sometimes a full 180 degrees to check behind them. They are always vigilant, keeping ears and eyes open for the approach of the larger predators who share their home. Cheetahs are at the bottom of the large carnivore pecking order. Built for speed rather than strength, they are easily overpowered by lions, leopards and hyenas. In a flat race, a cheetah can outmanoeuvre these larger animals, but when caught unawares, cheetahs are often ambushed by their more powerful cousins. Being full, and somewhat cumbersome, this pair were probably feeling particularly on edge. As one put its head down to drink, the other would keep watch. Alternating every minute or so in perfect, unspoken synchronicity.

Once both had slaked their thirst, they tiptoed away in single file, heads still turning, ears twitching, and eyes scanning the horizon for any potential threats.

We watched until they disappeared into the dappled light of the bushes. The whole encounter had only lasted five minutes, but the details were etched so clearly in my mind. My first sighting of cheetahs and the animals were every bit as beautiful as I had imagined.

The cheetah sighting, while memorable and unexpected, didn't compare to my first sighting of a leopard.

It was a month after we had arrived, and we had a few days off to prepare for our first set of written tests. A few of us decided to spend the night at the nearby bar to have a change of scenery and get to know the local area.

The bar was located in the middle of nowhere on a neighbouring reserve. Like any good bush bar, it was open-air. It had a thatched roof but no walls, so it was open to the wilderness. When we arrived, the place was deserted. We heard the bar was heaving on a weekend, filled with local guides, wildlife researchers and reserve workers meeting up to exchange their bush stories over steak and beers.

This being a Wednesday, we had the place to ourselves. With no other punters in, the manager had given most of the staff the night off, so it was just three of us and the barman, and his faithful Jack Russell terrier.

The bar was a couple of hours drive from the guiding school, so we had booked rooms to stay the night. While the barman set to cooking our steaks, we found our rooms to freshen up. After changing and putting on mosquito repellent, I walked the short distance past the swimming pool, along a dimly-lit flagstone pathway to the bar. I didn't have my torch with me, but the solar lanterns that lined the pathway were enough to find my way.

I perched myself on a stool at the bar. My mouth watered as a sizzling steak was put down in front of me. A fillet the size of my face – cooked medium rare with a pepper sauce – sat on an otherwise naked plate. The chef was not there, and the barman's culinary skills were limited to the preparation of meat. But I didn't mind. With steak as good as this, you don't need anything else. I ordered a Castle lager, the famous South African beer, and tucked in.

As I set my knife and fork down, having cleaned my plate, we plunged into darkness.

"Power cut," the barman explained. "They happen often here, you'll get used to it."

My eyes started to adjust to the blackness. I could just make out the barman rummaging underneath the bar. He emerged holding a single candle. He pulled a lighter from his pocket and lit the wick. A faint glow grew and, before long, we sat in a halo of soft, orange light.

With sight now restricted, my hearing took over as the primary sense. It was only then that I noticed the noise outside. The Jack Russell was barking frantically out by the pool. The barman called the dog, and it ran back into the bar, but his erect tail and ears indicated he was still interested in something outside. That something proved too powerful a pull, and the dog turned tail and headed straight back out, barking as he went.

"Most nights we have five dogs in here, charging all over the place, tripping everyone up," the barman told us. "He's probably feeling lost without the others and trying to make up for their absence."

Putting my feet up on the rail under the bar, I thought nothing more of it and ordered another Castle.

My repose was interrupted abruptly as the Jack Russell flew back into the bar, darting under my legs. This time, it was closely followed by another, larger dog. A brawl erupted on the floor next to my stool. Deep, guttural growls were coming from the two dogs as clouds of dust and fur were thrown up into the air. The larger dog straddled the Jack Russell, lunging at the smaller dog's neck. The smaller dog was on its back, kicking and biting. It was a real David and Goliath battle with the little dog putting up a heck of a fight. In the dim light of the candlelit bar, I couldn't make out the colour or breed of the other dog. Frozen to my seat, I watched the events unfold in slow motion. I was only vaguely aware of the sounds coming from behind me, which were muffled as if I was wearing headphones.

Then, as if with a snap of a hypnotist's fingers, the room came into sharper focus again. The commotion was deafening. I felt a tug on the back of my shirt, but I couldn't move a muscle. Instinctively, I knew I should stay completely still.

The barman, in a blur of movement, came flying over the top of the bar. His foot thrust forward and struck the larger dog on the backside - one, two, three times. There was a growl, then a snarl as the animal turned to face the barman.

Only then did my brain finally register the beast before me. Its flattened head and small round ears, the long, slender tail with a white tip. Along its flank, I could make out rosette-like patterns in the fur.

That is no dog, I realised. *That's a leopard!*

Bravely, the barman continued to shout and kick at the leopard until it climbed off the dog. Then with its belly to the ground, it slunk out of the bar, disappearing into the shadows, back in the direction it had come.

Splash! Apparently, the leopard had forgotten about the pool.

Then, silence.

I turned to face my friends. To my surprise, they were both standing up on the bar.

"Jeez, Rosie. Why didn't you get up here? We were shouting at you, but you just sat there!" I hadn't even heard them. I was still struggling to make sense of what I had seen. I told them I hadn't initially realised it was a leopard.

"What on earth did you think it was?" One of them asked.

"A big dog," I replied, sheepishly. They both looked back in disbelief.

The barman examined the Jack Russell. The dog escaped with only two tiny scratches under his neck.

"Jack Russells are hard as nails," the barman remarked while scratching the dog's head. "Why can't you pick on something your own size?" he joked whilst the dog continued to make every attempt possible to chase off after the leopard. "Right, I am going to lock this dog in the kitchen, then we better do a round of the grounds to check the leopard has gone."

I wasn't too keen on walking around in the darkness looking for a leopard, but I hadn't actually heard the leopard get out the pool again and I was picturing it doing laps and getting increasingly angry. *It probably is best that we know for sure it has left.*

With the dog safely locked away, the barman found a torch in the kitchen. Pulling a handgun from its holster on his belt, he told us to stay close behind him.

Cautiously, we checked the pool. Spotting a leopard-sized puddle on the far side, I was pleased to see the cat had managed to get out. I felt a wave of pity for the animal as I was quite sure leopards are not fans of swimming. Following the wet trail it left on the flagstones was easy. We tracked them along the path, right past the door to my room. *Had I walked past this leopard in the darkness earlier in the evening? What if it had attacked me instead of the dog?* My stomach knotted at the thought.

Satisfied that the leopard was no longer on the grounds, the barman searched for more candles to illuminate the bar, hoping the light would make it harder for the leopard to sneak in again. We searched the bar and kitchen, but couldn't find any.

The barman said he knew there were plenty of candles at the main house, a short drive away.

"Do any of you know how to use a firearm?" He asked.

We would be learning rifle handling later on in the course, but that wouldn't be for months. Two of us stood there shaking our heads like it was a stupid question. The third however, a Zimbabwean, smiled and replied, "Sure."

The barman handed over his handgun and told us to sit on the bar with the torch and keep flashing it about.

"If the leopard comes back, shoot at it," he said, matter-of-factly.

He can't actually leave us sitting here on the bar with a gun waiting for the leopard to come back, can he? I questioned. But he did.

"I'll be back in about 20 minutes" he said, as he jumped in his truck, speeding off. I listened to the sound of gravel spraying up from the tyres until he was out of earshot.

We were alone. Three student guides, only a few weeks into our training, with an aggravated, and now wet, leopard. It was a long 20 minutes. We sat in nervous silence, ears pricked to hear any sound that might suggest the leopard was back. Scanning the torch back and forth to light up any shadows that might harbour the ferocious cat. Only when we heard the crunching of gravel again, did we relax. The barman casually strolled in with a stack of candles and once they were all lit, the shadows evaporated and the bar felt warm and welcoming again.

The barman poured a round of shots to calm the nerves. No one was keen to go to bed just yet. We sat up for hours, reliving the events from each of our perspectives. However, once safely back in my room, after being escorted by an armed guard at the end of the night, I fell asleep quickly and deeply - and dreamt about swimming leopards.

In the morning, over eggs on toast, we discussed the factors that had led to such an unusual encounter. Having a leopard choose to come that close to humans, even under the cover of darkness, is incredibly rare. They are shy creatures and have a natural fear of people. There were several factors that played a role that night; if there had been more people in the bar, if the other dogs had been there, or if the lights hadn't gone out, the leopard probably wouldn't have entered the bar. Even so, for an animal to take such a risk, there is almost always an underlying cause. The leopard might be old or injured and unable to hunt wild prey, driving them to take risks out of sheer desperation. Sadly, in this case that turned out to be true.

A few weeks later, the same leopard returned to the bar, this time during daylight hours. It was apparent that she was in terrible condition, her body wasting away. The vet was called and she was euthanised. An autopsy revealed she had a large mass of rubber lodged in her stomach that was preventing her from eating. She was starving to death and, likely, had only a matter of days left to live. We will never know where the rubber came from or why the leopard had consumed it. The only thing we do know is the rubber came from humans, albeit unintentionally. As such, I felt it was unfair to put all the blame on her. However, the truth is, we were lucky that no one had been harmed. Sick and injured animals can be dangerous. This could have been a very different story.

"You realise no one is going to believe us," I said finishing off my last piece of toast with some apricot jam. Even I was not really convinced that it hadn't been a tequila-induced dream.

My friend smiled, "Don't worry, I have photographic evidence." He passed over his camera and I scrolled through the images of the wet leopard tracks and the tufts of golden fur on the floor. *How could I have thought it was a dog?* I scolded myself. *What kind of a guide am I going to make?*

I knew it would not be the last close encounter I would have - misadventures with wildlife were going to be my new normal - but I was also worried it wouldn't be the last time I questioned my abilities as a guide.

> *"In this story, there is a girl who is*
> *stubborn and strong-willed*
> *and who makes mistakes*
> *enough to fill an ocean."*
>
> *- Nikita Gill*[4]

Chapter 3

Learning Lessons the Hard Way

```
TEXT RECEIVED [13:03:2010, 10:18:58]
ROSIE: Hi Mum. I hit a hyena on the head with
a book last night...
```

One activity I loved during training was "sleep outs". Without tents or shelter of any kind, we would head into the bush and sleep beneath the stars. I studied astronomy at university in London, where you are lucky to see the moon on most nights let alone any stars. So, snuggled in my sleeping bag, watching the Milky Way illuminate across the sky and meteors flash past every few minutes was a truly magical experience. Fresh air on your face and the distant sound of a lion roaring - there's nothing like it. It's a humbling, yet liberating, experience everyone should try at least once in their lives - under the supervision of experts of course.

When I talk about sleep outs, most people think it is completely insane - a death wish. But provided you take certain precautions, it is relatively safe.

The rules for a sleep out are simple:

1. Keep a fire lit throughout the night.
2. Have two people awake at all times, undertaking the night watch.
3. When you are on night watch, you must remain standing and walk around, and use torches to regularly scan the surroundings for any potential danger.

From my own experience, I have now added an additional rule.

4. Keep a handy stash of small rocks nearby.

When setting up camp, the first job is to collect firewood and get the fire going. Next, pick your sleeping spot. The sleeping arrangements should be a tight circle radiating outwards from the fire, heads inwards, feet pointing out, like the spokes of a wheel.

Our first sleep out was at the end of the first term of training - a treat for passing our initial exams. After setting up camp and eating a dinner cooked on the coals of the fire, we were assigned into pairs and given a roster for the night watch. Each pair was responsible for waking up the next pair on the roster, making sure the new watchmen were up and walking around before retiring themselves.

I got the graveyard shift. With my roommate as my partner, our watch started at 1 a.m. and went on until 3 a.m.

At 12:55 a.m., I felt someone prod my shoulder. Groggily, I crawled out of my sleeping bag and headed to the fire. They had kindly put the kettle on the coals and I drank tea while they gave us some handover notes from their watch.

"We heard hyena calling about 20 mins ago from the east. But they weren't that close," one of them said. "Otherwise, it's been a quiet one. Hope you get some more excitement."

With that, they handed us the spotlight, and the night watch was ours. We scanned the bushes around our makeshift camp, no eyes shone back. We stood around the fire for a while, chatting in soft whispers so as not to disturb the others. I poured more tea and checked my watch, 1:15 a.m. *This is going to be a long watch.* I have never been good at staying awake at night. I need a solid eight hours to function.

I started pacing, making laps around the fire to keep myself awake. I was trying to recall the facts we had learnt that day about the charging speeds of different animals. I paced out ten metres and imagined what it would look like to have an elephant cover that distance in less than a second. My roommate moved over to the truck and parked herself on the bonnet with the spotlight. Every 15 minutes, she scanned the horizon. Still, no eyes shining back.

At around 2 a.m., my brain weary, I started questioning my memory of different charging speeds. *Surely it can't be right that a lion covers ten metres in less than half a second?* I went and grabbed the book I was reading before I had gone to sleep - 'Viewing Potentially Dangerous Animals.' It was one of our training textbooks that focused specifically on the more lethal animals you may encounter on safari. With my head torch on, I flicked through the pages until I found the one with the folded over corner. On it, a table with the different charging speeds of animals. I had marked the page as something I should probably try to memorise. *That will surely come up in the exam next month.*

Elephant: 11 metres per second. Buffalo: 15 metres per second. Lion: 20 metres per second.

Engrossed in the book - my mind reeling at the impossibly short times you have to react to a charging animal - I sat down on a camp stool by the fire. I only remembered I shouldn't be sitting down when a twig snapped in front of me.

I looked up. In the beam of my head torch, two ghoulish, red eyes glowed back at me.

It was a hyena, and it was standing inside the circle of sleeping bodies, no more than two metres from my face. Without thinking, I threw my book at the animal, hitting it square in the face. Startled, it turned tail and ran out of the circle of sleeping bodies, directly across my vacant sleeping bag.

A shout came from the truck, "Rosie, what are you doing?" My roommate had seen my shadow leaping about in the fire light.

"There was a hyena right here next to me," I shouted back. "I hit it on the head with my book and it ran in that direction. Shine the spotlight and see if it has gone?"

She turned on the spotlight and scanned the area. This time, there were eyes shining back from the inky darkness. As the beam from the spotlight scanned clockwise around the camp perimeter, more sets of eyes glared back. Four pairs in total. We were surrounded by hyena on all sides.

From inside a sleeping bag next to me, a muffled voice sounded.

"What is all the noise about?" It was the Serious One.

"We are surrounded by hyenas," I replied.

"So, throw some rocks at them until they go away," the voice said, sounding unamused and disinterested.

I grappled around at my feet, feeling for rocks. I hurled them in the direction of the hyena. The spotlight panned around, catching brief glimpses of the hyena, as they weaved and dodged out of the beam. We knew they were still approaching by the reflection of their eyes, glowing a satanic red. Woken by the commotion, a few people emerged from their sleeping bags to help with the rock slinging onslaught. It took five of us continuously lobbing rocks at the circling ghosts for ten minutes before the hyena finally gave up the game and melted into the darkness, whooping as they went.

Relieved, I sat back down in my chair. Only to jolt myself straight out again. *Don't sit down on night watch duty!* I admonished myself. *Had I not just learnt that important lesson?*

While my classmates were amused by the irony that I had used my Viewing Potentially Dangerous Animals book to fight off a hyena, they are not actually considered to be a particularly threatening animal. Hence why the Serious One was so unconcerned by the invasion. While they are perfectly capable of catching and eating a human, they don't generally consider us to be food. There have been rare reports of hyena grabbing an arm or head of a sleeping person, but attacks on someone who is awake are virtually unheard of. Hyenas are, however, curious and extremely bold. They were most likely drawn to our campsite by the smells of our dinner cooking earlier in the night and came to check if there were scraps for the taking.

In torchlight, their eyes shine red - as do most predators - making them appear demonic in the dark. But they have an undeserved reputation for being ugly and conniving. Hyenas are actually unbearably cute. With teddy bear faces and large, puppy dog eyes, they are far from scary or grotesque. They are intelligent, often comical, and seem to enjoy the company of people, making them enchanting to be around. Most importantly, they play a critical role in keeping humans safe, by removing carcasses and rotten flesh from the environment, so reducing the possibility of disease outbreaks. Despite occasionally having to throw books or rocks at them, interacting with hyena is one of my favourite pastimes.

Five months after the first sleep out, I had passed all my exams and, on paper, was now a fully qualified guide. I was able to take paying clients into the bush, unsupervised. But, I still had so many lessons to learn.

The second half of the Safari School training programme consisted of a six-month work experience placement to gain vital field hours to hone our skills. Rather than being placed in a lodge with safari-goers, I was placed with a research organisation that used qualified guides to take students and volunteers into the field to collect data on wildlife and the ecosystem. I tried to convince myself I earned this placement because I had excelled in my exams and had an aptitude for science, not because I couldn't be trusted with high-end tourists. Either way, it turned out to be a blessing. I loved the depth of knowledge a research project warranted. We spent months with the individual students and volunteers, instead of the few days you get with tourists. Our conversations went beyond the basics into detailed assessments about what we were observing in the field each day. As a result, I felt I could have a greater impact on my clients. And being a bit of a clown, formality doesn't come naturally to me, so the more relaxed atmosphere suited me perfectly. After only a few weeks at my placement, I knew I had found my niche in the industry.

The reserve where I was placed was in a remote part of northern South Africa. Compared to our training site, the reserve was vast and rugged. Apart from a handful of dams and rocky outcrops - known as koppies - the terrain was flat and thick with mopane trees. Navigating was challenging. Everywhere looked the same. Unless you could spot a couple of the koppies, it was difficult to know where you were and in which direction you were driving.

The reserve was also virtually devoid of humans. There were no lodges or tourist vehicles to stop and ask for directions and this lack of human activity also made for skittish and, sometimes, unfriendly wildlife. The elephants were particularly unaccommodating. When I first arrived on the reserve, my colleagues warned me to watch out for them as they were feisty and had a tendency to charge. Until then, I had only known even-tempered elephants. The thought of being charged by one made my stomach twist in knots. For the first few weeks, so focused on keeping alert for irate elephants, I barely thought about anything else whilst out on drive.

Elephants, surprisingly, are masters of concealment. In dense vegetation, an elephant can be completely invisible until you are right on top of it. While they can be incredibly noisy, in stealth mode an elephant moves silently. It is not unusual to drive by an elephant, only to become aware of its presence when you hear a thundering, disgruntled trumpet over your shoulder. When this happens and you are at close quarters, your body will jump right out of its skin.

There was also an animal on the reserve that was new to me - the black rhino. Until that point, I had only encountered white rhinos. Known as docile and peaceful, white rhinos are a pleasure to observe. In training, we had been close to them many times, both from the safety of the vehicle and also on foot. I felt relaxed and confident working around white rhinos. Black rhinos, on the other hand, are known to be cantankerous. And, having not met any yet, I only had a theoretical knowledge of them. But I was told there were hardly any black rhinos on the reserve, and they were shy and no one ever saw them.

During my first couple of weeks, I trained with another staff member, learning the roads and how to collect the research data. These supervised drives were uneventful. We saw neither elephants nor black rhinos, so I didn't get the chance to learn what to do if I came across either of them. I couldn't be supervised forever though, and the day came when I had to take students on a drive alone. My first "solo drive".

Needless to say, on this first solo drive, I encountered both an elephant and a black rhino.

I was out searching for, and failing to find, a couple of cheetahs. Not yet knowing the reserve very well, I was looking in all the wrong places, and soon, I was lost - really lost. Throughout the reserve, were hundreds of roads leading to nowhere. It had previously been a diamond prospecting site, and I suspect these were old roads from prospecting forays. I found it difficult to distinguish between these dead-ends and actual roads. So, I spent an exorbitant amount of time driving down a road for a kilometre or so only to find it petered out. I'd have to turn around and backtrack continuously, which got me increasingly frustrated. If there's one thing I really hate, it is being lost. Panic starts to well up inside me, I become melodramatic and make increasingly bad decisions - not a good response as a guide.

After taking several wrong-turns, I was flustered. Dusk was approaching and we were not allowed to drive at night on the reserve because of those troublesome elephants. The students in the back were waking up to our predicament and began making comments. I kept smiling and just waved off their concerns, determined to not let on that I was out of my depth. I have long known that a smile can be a secret weapon. Despite my crooked teeth, I was awarded a prize for having the 'nicest smile' in school and earnt the nickname "Smiles" - which was a vast improvement on "The Curly-Headed Monster" from my early childhood. I have since used this award-winning smile to my advantage, to win people over, reassure them, and to diffuse difficult situations. I hoped my prized grin could fool this bunch of students into believing I knew exactly what I was doing as well.

I eventually found a road I recognised and, to my horror, realised we were at least an hour-and-a-half drive from camp. It would be dark before we were back. If I struggled to navigate in the daylight, how on earth was I going to find our way home in the pitch black? And what if we bumped into one of those troublesome elephants? In an attempt to alleviate some of my rising panic, I radioed camp to give them an update of our location. *At least then they will have an idea of where to start searching for us if we get lost again.*

I didn't want to give away the alarm I was feeling, but I also wanted to impress on them that, in my mind, there was a very real possibility that we weren't going to make it home. However, there wasn't even a flicker of concern from the respondent on the radio.

"No problem, we'll save some dinner for you".

Is that it? I thought. *Don't they care that we could be lost forever in this stupid maze of a reserve?*

I was now angry and flustered - not a good combination when in the bush. A calm and clear head is needed to make sound decisions and remain safe. I was feeling neither calm nor clear-headed at this point.

I continued along the road in the direction I thought would take us home. It wasn't long before we came to a dry riverbed. The road cut right across the middle of it. In our old, battered Toyota Hilux trucks, crossing difficult terrain, like riverbeds, required getting out of the vehicle to manually lock the hubs on the front wheels, to ensure we were in four-wheel drive. Failing to do so, would get you stuck in the extremely soft sand of the riverbed. I dutifully locked the hubs, taking a moment while I was out of the truck to flash "the smile" and make a show of pretending all was fine for the benefit of the students.

We crossed the river with ease and after cresting the opposite bank, I jumped out and unlocked the hubs again. This distraction helped calm some of my nerves. *I really do know what I am doing*, I thought to myself. *I am a badass bush driver.* The smile on my face was becoming more natural, less forced.

Hopping back into the car, I saw the familiar grey shape of a rhino standing in the road 50 metres ahead of us. I turned to face the students in the back, my smile growing even wider.

"Look, rhino! I love rhino." This was going to make everything better. We hadn't seen any animals on our drive. Seeing a rhino was like hitting the jackpot. They were so rare on the reserve; I knew it was going to get me brownie points. That initial joy vanished in an instant though, as I saw everyone's eyes widen and I heard someone shout, "It's charging us!"

I spun round.

This was not a white rhino but a black rhino. Even worse, it was a mummy black rhino, hellbent on protecting her calf.

I quickly weighed up my options. If I reverse, I am going backwards into the riverbed. With my wheels unlocked, I will almost certainly get stuck. This was clearly not a sensible option. While I hadn't seen a black rhino before, we had learnt about them. They are short-sighted and nervous, often charging before actually knowing what the threat is. Once close enough to make out a truck, they will likely veer off at the last second. So, the best thing to do is stay still and try to alert them to your presence, intimidating them into changing course. I didn't seem to have any choice in the matter. My only real option was to stand my ground. Armed with only theoretical knowledge, I steeled myself to intimidate the one tonne of fury that was quickly bearing down on us.

More meekly than I had intended, I slapped the side of the truck and shouted a short, squeaky, "Hey!"

To my utter disbelief, it worked. She veered off to the right, crashing headfirst into the bushes. She had been less than 20 metres away when she turned and her momentum carried her well past us. I watched her disappear out of sight over my right shoulder, then turned to the girl in the cab next to me and grinned. *Look at me! I diverted a charging rhino.*

Unfortunately, as I was about to sing my own praise, I caught sight of the calf. *Oh crap*, I thought. In the commotion the calf had become separated from its mother. We were now a sitting duck between the two. *This cannot be a good thing.*

I heard branches cracking again on my right and the mother came exploding out the bushes 40 metres ahead of us. She had doubled back and was charging us again. A flicker of a memory from training flashed in my mind … *Black rhino often loop back and charge a number of times. Now I remember!*

This time, feeling empowered by my previous success, I banged the side of the truck more forcibly, shouting, "Hey, stop! No! Hey!"

This time she got within 10 metres of us, my heart was in my throat. I had no idea what happens to a vehicle when you are hit head-on by a rhino. And, I didn't want to find out. Gripping the steering wheel with my left hand bracing myself for the impact, I continued to bang the side of the vehicle with my right.

At the last second, she veered again, this time streaming past the bonnet and into the bushes on the left, where her calf had been standing seconds before.

There was silence in the vehicle. Everyone was holding their breath. Frozen to my seat, I dared only move my eyes from left to right, scanning the bushes, listening for the next explosion.

But, it never came.

The bushes remained quiet, the dust settled and I felt the tension lift. After a minute or so, there was a collective release of breath from the vehicle. A soft murmur came from the back of the truck as people roused from their state of immobilisation.

Adrenaline surged through my body. I felt alive. *Wow*, I thought. I hadn't panicked and I got us through it. *I can really do this. I am so hardcore.* I turned around to face everyone.

"Well, that was a bit bloody close wasn't it? But, wow, that was my first ever black rhino sighting. As you can see, they are a bit feisty!"

After checking everyone was ok, I crawled the truck forwards. Eyes flitting left and right still, just in case she decided to make another appearance. After 100 metres, satisfied she was gone, I pressed harder on the accelerator and cruised away. I grinned from ear to ear, *what a story to tell from my first solo drive.*

By now, dusk had set in and my eyes were taking a while to adjust to the low light. But my endorphins were pumping, so despite the low visibility, I was sailing along on a high. Any concerns about getting lost again or bumping into an elephant in the dark were forgotten. At least for the moment.

Suddenly, in the road loomed a giant, dark shadow. The bright ivory tusks glowing in fading light were the only thing giving it away.

It was one of those damned invisible elephants.

I slammed on the brakes and ground to a halt, spraying up gravel and dust. The elephant, that had been crossing the road, turned to face us. Head down, trunk flailing from side to side, he lolloped towards us.

This time, I did not have a riverbed behind me limiting my options, and I didn't have the nerve to stand my ground. I had seen the damage elephant can inflict on a vehicle and I was not in the mood to find out what this guy's intentions were. I threw the gear stick into reverse and stamped the accelerator down. We took off at pace backwards. Without taking his eyes of us, the elephant continued his intimidating march towards us.

Reversing on winding, bumpy roads, in diminishing light, while being pursued by an overly persistent elephant, is no mean feat. I had reversed more than 200 metres, and he was still homing in on us. *Ok, this is going to go on forever. I need to make a plan.* I saw over my shoulder the bush opening up on my right and in the clearing was a large baobab tree.

Notorious for their enormous girth, I thought the baobab tree might give us some degree of protection. I tucked us in behind the tree and turned the headlights off. Once stopped, I had visions of the elephant chasing us around the tree, like a scene in a Tom and Jerry cartoon. I felt foolish about my move, knowing that the elephant was infinitely more agile than our truck. If it came down to it, he would easily outmanoeuvre us in a game of cat and mouse. *Please leave us alone,* I implored. *Just keep on walking.*

The ball was entirely in the elephant's court now. I had played my hand and there was nothing I could do now except wait and see what his countermove would be. Metre-by-metre he closed the distance between us, giving nothing away as to what he would do next. The anticipation was agonising.

He drew level. I held my breath.

But, to my immense relief, he kept on going, straight past us and along down the road.

With the power of hindsight and experience, I now realise the elephant had not displayed any threatening body language. Perhaps, he followed us out of curiosity or maybe for fun. The reason he carried on going and didn't chase us round the tree was probably because he had simply grown bored with the chase once I stopped reversing. If I had just stood my ground in the first place, in all likelihood he would have left us alone. But at the time, all I knew was that the elephants on this reserve could be aggressive and I lacked the experience to read his behaviour and act accordingly.

Back in the truck, my left leg, poised over the clutch ready to make any evasive action necessary, was shaking violently. The adrenaline was now coursing through my veins uncontrollably. The girl next to me looked down at my leg.

"Are you shaking, Rosie?", she asked.

I laughed feebly. "Yeah. Don't tell anyone."

I didn't even turn to check on the other students this time. I was frazzled and just wanted to get back to camp. As soon as the elephant had reached what I considered to be a safe distance, I floored it in the direction of home.

It was now dark. The type of darkness you only get in the wilderness far from any light pollution. Millions of stars sparkled above us in the night sky, and my headlights were the only other illumination. Navigation was based on gut instinct alone. I drove faster than I should. Getting back to camp as quickly as possible was the only thing on my mind now. I turned a corner in the road and something darted through the beams of light fanning out from the front of my truck.

"Bear!", I blurted. *Bear?* I thought. *There are no bears in Africa. Rosie, you idiot.*

I turned to the girl next to me again, "Don't tell anyone I just said that either, please."

I slowed down and drove in a depressed silence the rest of the way home. *Did I really have what it takes to work in the African bush?*

> *"You have a dream, so chase it.*
> *Take a deep breath, chin up,*
> *pull your hair out of your face.*
> *It's time to fly."*
>
> *— Heidi Wilson*[5]

Chapter 4

~~Fake It~~ Practice 'Til You Make It

```
TEXT RECEIVED [20:08:2010, 09:12:03]
ROSIE: Hi Mum. I had a date with some snakes
yesterday…
```

Fortunately, what I lack in self-confidence, I make up for in stubbornness.

I have always been stubborn. As a young girl, this generally materialised in the form of refusing to do things I didn't want to do. When I was five years old, I hid under my bed for hours in protest after my dad laid out a dress for me to change into after school. I wanted to wear shorts that day. I hid so well and for so long, my family thought I was missing and called the police. The previous year, I was so adamant I didn't want my polio vaccination that, the second my mum got out the car at the doctor's surgery, I leapt into the front seat and locked the doors. Trapping myself in and my mum out. I was a strong-willed child. Once I had an idea in my head, it would be almost impossible to change my mind.

As adults, we have to be more flexible. We accept that we must do things we don't like to do, like pay our bills and put the bins out. Despite this, my stubbornness remains strong. While this sometimes still manifests in me refusing to do things, it is more commonly reflected in my pig-headed response to being told I can't do something instead. The more someone tells me I am crazy to try something, the more adamant I am to do it. And, when the person casting doubt is my own insecure self, my stubborn alter ego goes into overdrive.

Stubbornness is often seen as a flaw, especially in women. I say, nonsense. To get anywhere in this world you need to be a little stubborn. As Laurel Thatcher Ulrich, the Pulitzer Prize-winning American historian, said, 'Well behaved women seldom make history.' I am not suggesting you should be stubborn for petty reasons - not wanting to wear a dress is not a good reason to hide under a bed for five hours - but it pays to dig your heels in and fight sometimes. When stubbornness manifests itself as determination to succeed, it can be a powerful weapon to counter any self-doubt you might have.

In addition to being stubborn, I'm also an introvert. I tend to avoid asking questions or offering answers in public. I am happy to take a back seat, letting others lead or make decisions. Like many introverts, I tend to excel in written exams because the anonymity of that environment gives me the freedom to express my thoughts without the crippling fear of being wrong in public. But in this new career path I was forging, keeping quiet and hiding behind a pen and paper is not possible. Being vocal and making decisions is a critical part of the role. I was viewed as an expert and had a responsibility to use my knowledge to answer the questions my clients had and more importantly keep them safe. It was essential to find the confidence to speak up. I was outside my comfort zone, but I was discovering there was a real thrill in pushing these boundaries.

So many people fake it until they make it, but pretending to be better at something than I am doesn't work for me. It doesn't give me self-assurance, it breeds imposter syndrome and self-doubt. To have confidence, I need to have the knowledge and skills to back it up. This sometimes means having to work harder than the people around me until I have conviction in my own abilities in order to be as vocal as they are. This is where my stubbornness comes to the rescue. It gives me the determination to study and practice until I am as good as I need to be.

It was this stubbornness rather than self-confidence, my determination rather than natural ability, that meant I didn't give up, pack my bags, and go home after that cataclysmic first solo drive. Or, indeed, after any of the other disastrous days I have had on this adventure. Instead, I gritted my teeth and worked hard to develop the skills I needed not just to survive the wild, but overcome my insecurities as well.

Part of training as a guide is about learning to survive and be self-sufficient. This can range from knowing how to find food and water that won't make you sick, to being able to navigate using the stars or tell the time from the sun. You also learn practical skills necessary for a life in the bush. Skills like how to change a tyre in under five minutes - because more often than not you will get a flat tyre next to lions, and the less time you spend out of your vehicle with your back turned to them the better. A combination of necessity, experience and hard work mean I now have a range of skills and knowledge I never dreamed I would have in those early days. A range of skills that has helped me feel at home in the bush.

Reattach a prop shaft - sure. Instinctively park on a slope so you can always roll start the car if required - naturally. Fix the plumbing after a visit by the elephants - with my eyes closed. But there is one skill I never dreamt I would learn - catching some of the world's deadliest snakes.

It was somewhat ironic that my first night at guiding school included a close encounter with a cobra. Of all the creatures in the bush, snakes made me the most nervous. I had no experience with snakes at all. Unlike the big cats - which I had watched endless documentaries about - I knew nothing about their behaviour.

Before going to South Africa, I had swotted up on a few things, wanting to make a good impression and not wanting to fail in front of people. I learnt how to tell all the superficially similar antelope species apart, and the Latin names of the various mammals, along with their meanings or origins. I came unstuck, however, when I came across training materials on the snakes of Southern Africa. It was mind-blowing. There were so many species and, to a novice, they were extremely difficult to tell apart. The same species could be black, brown, grey, yellow or orange. Patterns were often no help either, the same snake could be spotted, banded or plain. The guidebook told me pupil shape, the texture of the scales and the number of scales on the head were all good indicators of species, *Well I'm sorry, but I am not sure I want to get close enough to a snake to take in that level of detail before having identified it.*

I decided to focus on the deadliest species. I figured with that knowledge I could keep myself safe at the very least. But reading about the speed with which a person can succumb to a black mamba bite gave me anxiety. I had to stop learning about them before I changed my mind about South Africa altogether. It was better to just pretend they didn't exist.

The calm displayed by our trainers on that first night with the cobra intrigued me though. Perhaps I shouldn't be so fearful after all. Over six months, the trainers had captured and removed numerous cobras at the farmhouse, and had also been called to remove one from the storeroom at a nearby lodge. It was apparent that being able to capture snakes safely might be a useful skill as a guide. And as having snakes in your house seemed to be quite a normal occurrence, it might also give me the confidence needed to deal with them. So, when the opportunity came up to do a training course at the local reptile centre, I seized my chance and signed up.

As part of the guiding course, we had already spent a full day at the reptile park learning everything you could imagine about snakes, from their evolution and anatomy to their reproductive strategies and venom types. Most importantly, we had learnt what to do if you or someone else is bitten by a snake. So, on the second outing to the park, we jumped right into catching snakes.

There were just two of us on the course, my infinitely braver Zimbabwean friend – the one who willingly accepted the handgun the night of the leopard in the bar – and myself. He had grown up catching snakes so for him it was more of a refresher course. For me, this would be the closest I had ever come to a snake in my life. Our trainer was an exuberant South African whose energy and enthusiasm for snakes was infectious. I instantly felt at ease with him and was brimming with excitement. For the moment, at least, I was full of confidence.

We started with the easy stuff, a puff adder.

The puff adder is Africa's fastest striking snake, capable of striking, piercing with its fangs, injecting venom and then retracting back to its coiled position again, all in under a quarter of a second. But its thick and squat body makes it a reluctant mover. Unlike most other snakes that will speed off at the approach of a human, the puff adder curls up and relies on its camouflage for concealment. To catch one, you simply need a large hook on the end of a long handle which you slide under the body of the snake and scoop it swiftly upwards. I managed this exercise with relative ease, calmly putting my suspended snake into a large tub and securing the lid tightly.

Snake one, tick.

Next up, a Mozambique spitting cobra. *Hmmm slightly more challenging*. These are much more agile snakes, and can spit their venom. Venom being sprayed onto skin is not too much of a worry. However, if it gets in your eyes, it causes a burning sensation leaving the victim, at least temporarily, blind. So for this exercise, we wore safety goggles.

Eye protection in place, they released the snake in a large, open area. We were instructed to run alongside the snake and grab it, this time with tongs rather than a hook. The tactic is to aim for the "sweet spot" on the snake – far enough from the head that it doesn't make the snake pull backwards and worm its way out of the tongs, but not so far that it is able to turn around and bite you. Depending on the size of the snake, this is normally around one third to halfway along its body length. When a snake is moving along in a straight line, this is simple to judge. But this is almost never the case when catching a snake. A snake that is moving along in the open is already removing itself from the situation. The snakes that need to be captured are the ones that are tucked under a bed, inside a cupboard, or perhaps, in the shower.

Once we understood the concept, it was time for a real-world scenario. I was taken to a shed and simply told someone had reported a snake inside. I was given no more information. I cautiously opened the door and found a room approximately three metres by three metres, packed with junk. I turned to the trainer, "Are you kidding me?"

"Look," he said matter-of-factly, "I just want you to be the most prepared you can be. Believe me, most times you are called to remove a snake it will be in a situation not dissimilar to this."

I peered into the dark clutter. My face, flushed with stress, fogged my safety goggles. I went to lift them off my face.

"Don't take your goggles off. You don't know if it is a spitting snake or not yet," the trainer warned.

Nodding my understanding, I wiped my brow with the back of my palm. I took a deep breath before methodically working my way through the room. I picked up each item of rubbish with the snake tongs, gave it a bit of shake to confirm the snake was not inside before removing it from the shed. A minute or so in, I lifted up a box that felt heavier than it should. Setting it down, I lifted the flaps with the tongs. Inside sat a small Mozambique spitting cobra, coiled in a tight ball. I looked at it for a while trying to judge where the sweet spot was in the tight coil. Giving it a gentle nudge in the belly, the coils released just enough for me to grab around the body with the tongs. Quick as a flash, I lifted the snake out the box and placed it in my pre-prepared tub, carefully closing the lid.

Snake two, tick.

This isn't so bad, I was thinking to myself. But so far, all the snakes I had caught had complied and were relatively small.

The hard stuff was yet to come.

I was taken to a small house at the back of the park where visiting volunteers to the Reptile Park stayed. At the doorstep to the house, I was told, "There's a snake somewhere in this house. Go find it and bring it out."

The house was not cluttered like the shed, but it was about four times the size, and had many nooks and crannies that could conceal the snake. I started my methodical search, working from room to room, carefully moving objects and looking under items to find the snake.

Almost ready to give up, I spied in the corner of the lounge, a large vase of dried flowers. It was about a metre high and opaque, which meant I could not see through it. I tapped the side of the vase and received a *shhhhh* in reply as the snake's scales rubbed against the stems of the dried flowers. Using my tongs, I removed the dried flowers. Then, I inched closer and closer until I could peer into the vase. This time it was not a small spitting cobra but an enormous, black-and-white striped, snouted cobra. The snake hissed, clearly unhappy with my intrusion.

Knowing I didn't need the safety goggles, I ripped them off my face in dramatic fashion. I took two deep breaths to steel my nerves before lowering my tongs inside the vase. By some miracle, I grabbed the snake in approximately the right place, and lifted it from the vase. It was significantly larger than the previous snake though and I was unprepared for the weight, struggling to lift it free of the vase with one arm. Using my left hand as extra support, I finally got the snake clear. Trembling, I could barely take the weight of the snake. In my panic, my earlier training flew out the window as I flung the snake into the tub, bent down to grab the lid and slammed it shut.

Over my shoulder, the trainer who had been watching just a metre or so away yelled, "No! What are you doing? Do you want to get bitten? Jeez."

He asked me to repeat back to him the steps for dealing with a large snake like a snouted cobra.

"Once you have it in the tongs, move it to an open area and while pushing the bitey-end away from you, pick up the tail, so not all the weight is being taken in your tong-holding arm," I recited, bashfully.

"And then?"

"Lower the snake into the tub and release the tongs slowly."

"And then?" He prompted.

"Wait until the snake has settled before putting on the lid."

"And why do we do that?" He asked.
"So you don't get bitten if it is trying to escape."

"Yes. Luckily, I was watching and could see it wasn't coming out. Otherwise, I would have stepped in. But I won't be there to look out for you when you are doing this on your own." I nodded, deflated by the admonishment. "Ok, you are going to have another go."

With that, I was sent outside while the snake was hidden again. I paced around kicking myself for being stupid and trying to not think about the fact that I could very easily have been bitten by a snake whose venom is almost as potent as a black mamba. I recited the rules over and over in my head.

The second time, I found the snake quickly. It was inside a pillowcase on one of the beds. I managed to shake it free, and this time, followed the rules, picking up the tail to take some of the weight. It felt wrong to hold the snake's tail in my bare hand, but I struggled less under the weight of the bulky snake. I carefully lowered the snake into the tub and let go of the head end. The snake immediately shot out the tub. Startled, I jumped backward. Behind me the trainer barked, "Grab it quickly, before it goes under the sofa."

I regained control of the snake and lowered it back into the tub. Again, it shot out. We repeated this six or seven times before the snake eventually tired and coiled on the floor of the tub. I slowly put the lid down, this time probably more slowly than necessary. I stepped back, trembling from the exertion.

"Right, let's have one more go."

I shot the trainer a look of disbelief.

"Really? Please, no. I am exhausted," I pleaded.

"I can't sign you off until I am sure you can do it right every time," he replied, the deadpan look on his face told me he wasn't joking.

He briefly disappeared to get a different snake, one that was fresh and feisty no doubt. Then the stage was set once again, and I was sent into the ring for one final round.

Before I got a chance to catch the snake, however, it found its way under a wardrobe, wedging itself between two panels of wood. There was no way to get the snake out without taking apart the wardrobe. If we did that, we wouldn't have time to complete the other training exercises required to pass the course. So, much to my relief, I was off the hook.

While the trainer roped in some other staff from the park to dismantle the wardrobe and retrieve the snake, we had 15 minutes to wolf down lunch and rehydrate. With this first chance to take a step back and breathe, exhaustion came over me in a wave. The adrenaline and stress were too much, and tears welled in my eyes. My Zimbabwean friend put his arm around my shoulders and gave me a squeeze.

"Don't worry Rosie. You're doing great."

"I can't do it," I replied. "I don't think I want to catch snakes after all."

"Of course you can," he smiled sympathetically. "You know he's only pushing you so hard because he's got the hots for you, right?"

"Don't be ridiculous." I pulled a face at him. But as I turned to walk away, the briefest of smiles broke on my face, and the tears evaporated.

Unfortunately, the afternoon was progressively more difficult. We took a quick break from the venomous snakes to learn how to catch pythons. This should have offered some respite, but, inexplicably, I found pythons even more stressful than cobras. The python I had to catch was enormous, I was sure it weighed more than me. It was also surprisingly fast and very "bitey". Worst of all, there were no tools for catching pythons, your bare hands were all you got. As strange as it may sound, for a wildlife enthusiast, I don't really like touching animals at the best of times. I enjoy observing wildlife, but I don't have a desire to pet animals. Grabbing the head of a giant python, while it hisses and shows off its razor-sharp teeth, was especially unappealing.

The first time, I was so hesitant that the trainer intervened, grabbing my hands and shoving them onto the head of the python. Unfortunately, as he did so, I yanked my hands free, allowing the snake to sink its teeth into the trainer's hand. It wasn't a serious bite, and he pulled free straight away. But, blood was drawn, and I was mortified. After he was patched up, he asked me to try again. As much as I tried, my body refused to move, my feet were frozen to the spot, and I simply watched my python start to haul its colossal bulk up a nearby tree.

"Well, go on then, get up the tree and get it back," the trainer said, pointing to the tree.

Um...Yeah, no. I shook my head. I wasn't grabbing it on the ground, I sure as hell was not climbing up a tree after it. I can barely climb trees at the best of times, let alone one with an enormous python in it. Noticing the look of horror on my face, my Zimbabwean friend came to my rescue and quickly scaled the tree and descended with my snake. The ease at which he swung about in the tree was reminiscent of Tarzan. He got his tick next to 'python catching,' I still hadn't.

By now I had stopped speaking. I knew if I opened my mouth even a tiny bit the tears would come flooding back. I kept my lips pursed tightly shut and breathed deeply through my nose. *In for three, out for three. In for three, out for three.* Out of sheer grit and determination, on my third attempt I got my tick next to python catching.

Finally, we were off to the snake pit for the last exercise of the day. The snake pit was a large hole in the ground, surrounded by a brick wall topped with an electric fence. Spectators could stand around the edge and safely peer down at the demonstrators inside the pit as they contended with mambas and boomslang, Africa's most venomous snakes.

Inside the pit were two trees, in the branches of which sat several snakes. This lesson was about catching arboreal, or tree-loving, snakes. First, we practiced with the boomslang. While being Africa's most venomous snake, the venom is extremely slow acting. You have days to live as opposed to the hours you get with a mamba. They are also extremely reluctant to bite. Being bitten by boomslang in the wild is virtually unheard of. The tricky part, though, is that arboreal snakes curl and knot themselves around branches. You have to slowly untangle them with the tongs and your free hand, one curl at a time with your arms above your head and your neck craned up towards the sky.

I managed to capture the boomslang with some degree of success. The snake didn't make life too difficult for me. However, it was a time-consuming process unravelling the snake from the branches. By the time I had completed the task, my arms were like lead and I could barely lift them above my head.

Unfortunately, I had to. Next up, the black mamba - the most feared snake in Africa.

Black mamba venom is potent and works fast. Their bodies are long, up to four metres, and they are lightning-fast. Catching them is extremely difficult and dangerous and should be avoided if at all possible. But black mambas are often found in the rafters of houses. In the event that we were confronted with no other option, we needed to learn how to deal with one in this kind of situation – where the snake is wrapped around something above your head.

The same principles applied as with the boomslang - a slow, methodical process of unwinding the snake from the branches, starting at the tail, until you could lift it from the tree. Despite having managed with the boomslang, the mamba was significantly harder. My arms felt instantly weak and shaky with the effort of holding them above my head. Tension in my neck restricted my movements. I had to keep dropping my head to relieve the cramping. Unlike the boomslang that had been compliant and patient, the mamba kept crawling deeper into the tree and jerking its head about. Every time it did this, I flinched and let go. The snake would, quick as a flash, coil back up the length I had already painstakingly unwound, setting me back to square one. It took every inch of my strength and determination to keep going. Every time either the trainer or my friend urged me on with words of encouragement, the tears, again welling in my eyes, got closer to spilling out. After more than half an hour of the tortuous exertion, I eventually lifted the snake free from the tree.

A cheer erupted from above me, I suddenly realised there was a crowd of tourists watching. I was grateful I hadn't known they were there before. The added pressure would have been too much to bear. After I received the go-ahead by the trainer, I put the snake back in the tree. I turned around and walked off without saying a word. I was unable to look anyone in the eye for fear of exposing my tears and the weakness they reflected.

The day was done. I had succeeded in each task and was presented with a certificate acknowledging that I was trained in the capture and safe release of dangerous snakes. All I managed was a strangled "thank you" as I was handed my certificate. I slunk off to the car leaving the Zimbabwean and trainer to exchange snake stories for ten minutes.

Back home, I went straight to my room and closed the door. Despite the early hour, I got into bed. It was silly to be so upset. I had achieved something extraordinary and should have been proud. But, I wasn't. I was upset because I had found it so hard. I had this fantasy of being a tough bush girl, a girl of the wild. But it turned out I wasn't as tough as I thought. Exhausted, I fell asleep before it was even dark. I slept fitfully throughout the night, snakes rearing at me in my dreams.

I woke the next morning to a text message. It was from the trainer.

```
TEXT RECEIVED [20:08:2010, 06:04:03]
SNAKE GUY: What are you doing this weekend? Fancy
catching up?
```

I can't have been that pathetic yesterday then! I thought. The combination of 13 hours sleep and this text message helped relieve some of the trauma of the previous day. I picked up the certificate I had left on my bedside table. *Certified Snake Catcher, that is pretty badass. If I can do this, then surely, I can do anything?*

> *"Her messy hair a visible*
> *attribute of her stubborn spirit.*
> *As she shakes it free, she smiles*
> *knowing wild is her favourite color."*
> — *J. Iron Word*[6]

Chapter 5

Misadventures of the Venomous Kind

```
TEXT RECEIVED [05:03:2014, 17:05:45]
ROSIE: Hi Mum. Had to cut open the sofa today
to retrieve a black mamba...
```

After finishing my work experience placement, I spent a couple of years freelancing for various research projects around South Africa. One of the jobs involved following wild dwarf mongoose, Africa's smallest carnivore, around all day long. At the time, I was the only person at the site, and my primary role was to keep track of the mongoose groups until the next research projects began in six months' time. The mongoose were on a tiny, private nature reserve. There were no lion, elephant, rhino or buffalo, so it was considered relatively safe for walking around on foot – which is the only practical way to study a mongoose not much bigger than a gerbil. For long stretches of the time, there weren't many tourists, so I mostly had the reserve to myself. I would sometimes go more than two weeks without speaking to another human, only conversing with the many animal friends I made while pottering around the bush on my own.

It was a period of time where I had the opportunity to be fully immersed in my wild surroundings. I was just starting to feel confident about my abilities in the bush. This, combined with the fact that I wasn't responsible for anyone else, nor was there anyone around to see me make mistakes, meant that I could push the boundaries and test my skills. I explored with the curious mind of a child, critically examining everything I observed – every mark in the sand and every noise in the air. It was a steep and rewarding learning curve.

Because I was alone, and often accompanied by my trusting mongoose friends, wildlife largely ignored me. The birds and antelopes seemed to assume that if the mongoose weren't alarm-calling at my presence, I wasn't a threat. As such, animals came much closer to me than they normally would have. Many would feed within touching distance of me as I sat captivated on a rock.

Not all the animals were benign, though. While there weren't the major dangers like elephants and lions, I did have other creatures to contend with. My house was built into the banks of the mighty Olifants river. On the river side, the façade was almost entirely glass providing panoramic views of the river. On the rear side, the house had been contoured into the ground, so that a grassy lawn ran all the way from the driveway up onto the roof. At night, hippos - reportedly, Africa's deadliest mammal - would graze on my roof. I would often have to negotiate them in the driveway whenever I came home after dark.

Leopards were also prevalent, and I frequently bumped into them or their kills while walking through the reserve. More disconcertingly, I often found their tracks overlaying mine as I backtracked home at the end of an observation session with the mongooses. I also regularly walked into large crocodile, basking out of the water. I once disturbed one while it was stealing a kill from a leopard. On seeing me, the crocodile dropped the quarry and disappeared back into the water. I prefer leopards to crocodiles so I was glad the leopard didn't lose its hard-earned meal.

While we weren't supposed to have any lions on the property, one morning I found the pug marks of two male lions right outside my house. Curious as to whether they were still on the reserve or simply passing through, and a little bit nonchalant about the dangers, I trailed them on foot for the rest of the day. I never found them, although that doesn't mean they didn't find me, of course.

Being on foot and moving around quietly, also meant I had far more snake encounters than one might normally have when living in the bush. Fortunately, having befriended the snake handling trainer, I had spent a lot of time around snakes, and my earlier fear had been replaced by fascination. As I grew more comfortable with them, I became more competent and confident at catching them, even acquiring my own snake catching equipment so that I was ready to capture one whenever the need arose. I quickly became the designated snake catcher wherever I worked and I seemed to attract snakes everywhere I went.

One day comes to mind, when I was out looking for mongoose and I trod on two snakes in quick succession. The first was a large python crossing the road. It was so big, it was unfathomable that I didn't notice it. I was probably contemplating which bird I could hear calling, my head in the sky, when I stepped on its tail and felt a sharp tug from under my foot. I apologised profusely but it shot me a disgusted look and slid away. Half an hour later, while traversing over some rocky terrain, I was still feeling bad about the python when I noticed the ground under my left foot felt odd. *That is quite a soft and muscular feeling*, I thought, *I don't think my foot is on a rock.* I looked down and saw a fat puff adder beneath my foot. I leapt, catlike, both upward and back, away from the snake, landing a couple of metres away. I am terrible at jumping. At school, despite being captain of the netball team, I was continuously ridiculed for not being able to jump either vertically or horizontally. It was a miracle I ever competed for a ball under the shooter's circle in a game of netball and my long jump attempts looked more like a nosedive. It seems all it takes to get air like Michael Jordan is to stand on one of Africa's deadliest snakes.

A safe distance away and reassured I wasn't bitten, I took a second to compose myself, then grabbed the camera that was permanently strapped to my back. I belly-crawled back towards the snake to take photos. She was stunning and beautifully camouflaged – it was no wonder I hadn't seen her. Despite being squished by my clumsy footing, she obliged my photoshoot for a few minutes before eventually moving off into some bushes to hide.

Weeks later, I was marching along the road to get to the mongoose den before they woke up, when I heard a noise that I couldn't identify. It sounded like a tyre deflating, but not just an ordinary car tyre, something much bigger, like a tractor tyre. Intrigued, I kept walking in the direction of the noise, running various possibilities through my head as to what could be making such a noise. I rounded the corner and was shocked.

On the road, an enormous python was being harassed by two honey badgers. To this day, I don't know which animal was making the extraordinary noise, but I suspect it was the badgers as they make a range of strange vocalisations. Honey badgers have a reputation for being the toughest animal in the bush. Unafraid of anything, they will even take on lions and buffalos, two creatures few dare to mess with. They are also notorious snake hunters, having a natural immunity to even the most potent of cobra venoms. In this battle, they definitely had the upper hand. Despite the python's superior size, they were harassing the snake, which was making every attempt to escape.

On seeing me round the corner, the honey badgers abandoned their snake victim, turned, and ran straight at me. This is the only occasion I have been in the vicinity of a snake, yet been more scared of another animal. To have two honey badgers run straight at you, armed with nothing more than a clipboard and a camera, is utterly terrifying. I did the only thing I could think of and put the clipboard in front of my legs as a shield, hoping I might be able to bat the badgers away. I knew it was a ludicrous plan, but it was all I had. Fortunately, the badgers split, and passed by either side of me, running up the road in the direction I had just come. The python, seeing its opportunity to escape, flung itself down an old aardvark hole in the side of a termite mound, to recover from the ordeal. I stood in silence for a few moments, marvelling at what I had just witnessed.

After a couple of years freelancing, I had gained enough experience to consider myself competent, even to my self-discerning eyes. As a result, I landed a job as the manager of a research project. It was run by the same organisation that I had undertaken my work experience placement with, but on a different reserve near to Kruger National Park. This reserve had the big five - lion, leopard, elephant, rhino and buffalo - so most of my work was done in a vehicle. But I still had frequent snake encounters - this time they were nearly all in our house.

It was an old farmhouse, similar to the one at guiding school. This time, I was the Serious One, responsible for the safety of nine employees and as many as 20 volunteers and interns. And, unfortunately for me, snakes, particularly Mozambique spitting cobras, were regular visitors to the house. At least once a month I would hear a shout, "Rosie! There's a snake." One summer, things really got out of control. I call it the *Summer of Snakes*.

There must have been favourable weather conditions or something going on because that summer there were an incomprehensible number of snakes. I was catching at least one cobra a week, often coming home from an exhausting day in the field to find everyone standing outside the house waiting for the snake catcher to return because a cobra was in the kitchen, or crawling up the side of someone's mosquito net. One day, I dislocated my shoulder and drove myself to the hospital 90 minutes away, only to arrive back at the house to see everyone standing outside.

"Rosie, glad you are back. There's a cobra on the verandah." I sighed, but dutifully caught and removed the snake, one-handed, while the other arm was in a sling.

The most ridiculous spate of snakes happened one evening when I arrived home, sweaty and famished, after a long day in the field. Before heading to dinner, which was already on the table, I went to drop off my equipment in my room. I opened the door and almost trod on a cobra. Luckily, my tongs were hanging on the wall right by the door. I grabbed them and swiftly scooped up the snake. It had now become so routine, I barely thought about it. I popped it in the snake tub and put the tub on the back of the truck, drove five kilometres into the bush and dumped it out. The snake was not impressed with being so unceremoniously chucked out, and promptly spat its venom all over me. Luckily, I had been wearing my safety goggles. When I got back to the house, I jumped straight in the shower to wash the venom off and prevent me inadvertently rubbing any in my eyes.

Emerging from the shower, I finally headed to dinner, sure that everyone had started without me. As I walked to the dining room, I came across another cobra on the pathway. I rolled my eyes, sighed and quickly jogged back to my room to get the snake catching equipment. This one was not keen on being caught and took me a couple of attempts to grab the sweet spot, the snake spraying me with venom in the process. Again, I drove the snake into the bush, this time five kilometres in the opposite direction, returned, and showered again to wash away the venom.

Having had my second shower in the space of 20 minutes, I was now ravenous and could already hear the plates being cleared away. *They better have bloody saved me some*, I thought to myself, slightly irritated that while I was saving everyone from deadly snakes, they were eating cottage pie and probably hadn't even noticed I was missing. Walking back along the pathway to the dining room, I stopped dead in my tracks.

YOU HAVE GOT TO BE KIDDING ME!

There, curled up, was yet another cobra. Much bigger than the previous two, I started to wonder if she was a female and the others had been her offspring. Stubbornly, I refused to go back to get the tools again, and I refused to be spat on, only to shower again. I was hungry and wanted my dinner. I grabbed a broom that was resting against the wall and, with a sweeping motion, chased the snake up the steps, across the driveway and into the bushes on the far side of camp.

This is not a recommended way to remove a snake, and she, no doubt, returned only hours later, but I had had enough snake catching for one night. I needed my cottage pie.

Incredibly, this wasn't the only day that month I had multiple snakes to deal with at the same time.

The volunteers and I were returning to the house from brunch at a nearby lodge, an indulgent treat after a rare night of heavy partying. I was locking up the minibus, the hungover volunteers shuffling toward the house like zombies, full of fried eggs and bacon, when I heard a sound that made me stand up and take notice. Even with a foggy head, a girl of the wild is always alert to warning sounds in the bush.

Above the door to the house was an electricity cable that ran to the solar panels. Along this cable, a pair of red-headed weaver birds had hung their elaborate grass nest. I thought it was ingenious. Instead of a tree, their normal nesting location, this seemed to be safe from most arboreal predators. But the noise I heard was the frenetic alarm call of the weaver birds which could only mean one thing - a snake was near their nest.

"Guys, stop! I think there's a snake above you," I called out.

I ran over and, sure enough, there was a stunning emerald green boomslang working its way, like a trapeze artist, along the wire from the rafters of the house to the nest. The adult weaver birds were trying in vain to turn it back and save their babies who were chirping inside the nest.

Assessing the situation, I decided no one was in immediate danger and so went into guide mode. I suggested people take out their cameras and began to narrate what was unfolding before us. Ignoring the dive-bombing it was being subjected to, the snake made its way into the nest. There was nothing more the parent birds could do, the result was inevitable.

The nest soon fell silent.

I called to one girl, who had gone to fetch her camera, to close her window. Her bunk bed was just the other side of the window from where the boomslang slithered. I didn't want it coming in through the window after it had finished raiding the nest.

No sooner had I called the instruction out, I heard a squeal from inside the same window.

"Rosie! There's another one in here!"

I went running into the bedroom and saw, to my utter disbelief, another emerald boomslang curled around the curtain rail of the window. *What are the chances?* I thought. *Two male boomslang* – only the males are an emerald green – *within inches of each other.*

This one I couldn't leave. It was less than a metre from the girl's pillow. I sent someone to get my tools and I started to climb the bunk bed ladder.

Once on top of the bunk bed, I had very limited room to manoeuvre. There wasn't room between the bed and ceiling to allow me to stand upright. And the snake was so close that I couldn't hold the snake tongs out straight in front of me, I had to angle my arms like a contortionist to get in any sort of position to grab the snake. If I stepped backwards, I would fall straight off the bed down to the concrete floor. And maintaining balance was demanding on the soft and wobbly foam mattress. It was a precarious situation to say the least. To make matters worse, I now had an audience of 20 people gawking, cameras ready. All the rules of catching snakes had gone out the window. The only thing going in my favour was that it was a boomslang and therefore not very "bitey".

I stood legs astride giving myself the most stable foundation possible, while hunched over like a granny to avoid banging my head on the ceiling. The tub was ready in front of me. I knew I had one chance, otherwise all hell was going to break loose with a scared snake scrambling around a dormitory full of bunk beds, suitcases and, of course, the 20 spectators.

Satisfied the snake wasn't coiled around the curtain rail, merely sitting on top of it, I took my chances and targeted a spot that was, hopefully, close enough to the head that I could prevent it lunging at my face. In the moment, I had forgotten that boomslang, being an arboreal snake, always headed upwards when feeling threatened, even when there is nowhere to head. The second I grabbed the snake, it shot upwards with all its might. This was a large male, much stronger than the small female I had manipulated in the tree during my capture course. The force of the snake flying upwards threw me backwards, nearly knocking me off my feet. Using all the strength I could muster, I managed to regain control as I threw the snake into the tub, slamming down the lid with my left hand. The memory of being yelled at in my capture course flashed back in my head. I should have waited for the snake to settle before putting on the lid. I lifted the lid off again to check I hadn't squished the snake. Thankfully, the snake was not pulverised and was, remarkably, still in the tub. Quick as a flash, I slammed the lid down again.

I looked round and saw a sea of faces gawking back at me, mouths agog like goldfish.

"Phwoor! That was a bit tricky," I said. *Understatement of the year.* I passed the tub down to one of my colleagues and climbed down the ladder. Taking back the tub, I headed straight for the truck. I wanted to get away from all these people as quickly as possible so they couldn't see how much I was shaking. *I am not doing something like that again,* I thought to myself.

Fortunately, that thought stayed with me when, a few weeks later, I heard a scream from the other side of the house.

"Aaargh! Snake."

I picked up my tools and went to investigate. One of my colleagues came bursting out of her bedroom door onto the verandah.

"I just stepped over a black mamba," she said. "It's gone under the sofa." She pointed to a dirty, brown velour sofa that lived on the verandah.

People often claim they have seen a black mamba regardless of what the snake looks like - always fearing the worst. So, I took her observation with a pinch of salt and nudged the sofa forwards. But sure enough, the unmistakable face of a black mamba was staring back at me. Black mambas get their name from the intense, black colour of the inside of their mouth. That, along with their ironically coffin-shaped head, is a harbinger of death. Of all snakes in Africa, the black mamba's venom will kill you the fastest, potentially in under an hour, if medical treatment is not provided.

I didn't have any ambitions of trying to catch the mamba; I remembered our sage warning during training that it was incredibly risky to do so unless really experienced. However, I thought I might at least be able to scare it into leaving of its own accord. I tipped the sofa over onto its front. Unfortunately, this had the exact opposite of my desired effect, and the snake disappeared inside the belly of the sofa through a hole in the fabric.

That's it, I thought. *I am calling the experts.*

The reptile park offered a complimentary service removing snakes from homes in the local area. I put in a call and they were happy to come assist. We took turns keeping watch, to make sure the snake didn't move, until they arrived.

First, they assessed the scene and tried, as I had, to agitate the snake out by tipping the sofa over again. A snake emerged, but it was not the black mamba. A small and harmless spotted bush snake appeared and promptly slithered away.

"Rosie, did you call us out for a spotted bush snake?" they questioned me.

"No, come on guys. You know me. I swear on my life there is a large mamba inside the sofa," I protested. However, doubt was creeping in. *Could I really have mistaken that tiny green snake for the legendary mamba?* No, I was certain I hadn't made such a rookie mistake. *The mamba was real.*

After about ten minutes of postulating, the professionals turned to me and one said, "we have to cut the sofa open. Do you give us permission to do that?"

"Yes, of course," I replied. They could take an axe to it for all I cared. Whatever was required to get rid of the snake.

I handed over my penknife and they started to cut the fabric away from the back of the sofa. After only a few cuts they saw the snake and a weight lifted from my shoulders. *Ok, I was not imagining things.*

It took the two professionals 40 agonising minutes of careful extraction to bring the snake under control and safely tubbed.

"Sorry about the sofa," one said. I laughed, looking at what was now a large pile of worn fabric and wood. "Do you want to come watch the release?" he asked.

"Absolutely."

We drove a few kilometres down the road. My colleagues and I stood on the back of the truck to watch from a safe distance as the professionals prepared to release the snake. One of them lifted the lid of the tub and the snake shot at least a metre-and-a-half into the air. Luckily, they had been expecting it and were standing well back with the lid as a shield. What they hadn't expected was that the snake would promptly make a beeline for our truck.

"No, oh shit!" one of them shouted. Snakes have a habit of coiling up inside car engines – an even more challenging removal than from a sofa. Fortunately, this one wasn't interested in the car, and passed right under the vehicle and into bushes on the other side. We all sighed in relief.

The hero snake-catchers left and we headed back to the farmhouse. I ordered the sofa to be chopped up for firewood for our next braai. From now on, I vowed, I would only have furniture that couldn't harbour deadly snakes.

> *"Some are born to play it safe.*
> *Others are born to live it wild."*
> *- Nikki Rowe*[7]

Chapter 6

Misadventures of the Terrorist Kind

```
TEXT RECEIVED [15:10:2010, 16:43:50]
ROSIE: Hi Mum. I drank a dead monkey...
```

I like to think I have good karma with most wildlife. I am calm and respectful around animals and, in turn, I've been blessed with many wonderful encounters. At least this is true for larger mammals. My relationship with the smaller creatures of the world has been less amicable.

On a bush walk, I'll be the one to stand on an ants' nest and be covered by enraged, biting ants. I have stripped down to my underwear on more than one occasion in an attempt to rid myself of what feels like a thousand needles injecting my skin with fire. If it's not ants, then it will be ticks. I once sat covered head to toe in tiny ticks for 40 minutes because my car had broken down next to a hyena den. Being surrounded on all sides by curious hyena, I was unable to get out and brush the ticks off. Evidently, just before driving to the den, I had walked through a bush, and shaken loose its entire population of ticks. I only noticed once I was stuck in my seat waiting for a rescue vehicle. While I had time to kill, I picked the ticks off, one-by-one, tossing them out the window. But after 40 minutes, my khaki trousers were still speckled black with the tiny parasites. It is a miracle I have never had tick bite fever.

If it's not ticks, it's mosquitoes. For whatever reason, mosquitoes love my blood. It's often the case that, at the end of an evening, my companions have hardly noticed the presence of mosquitoes, and I look like I have shingles. It doesn't matter how much repellent I put on, or what clothes I wear, they will always find a way to my skin. According to folklore, the vitamin B in Marmite helps deter mosquitoes. But I eat Marmite nearly every day and based on my own scientific observations, I have seen no reduction in my allure to these irritating creatures. Luckily, I have only had malaria once.

Next up on the list of tiny creatures that love to hate me, spiders. If there's a spider in the house, I'll be the one that gets bitten. Unfortunately, I'm particularly susceptible to the toxins in spider venom. A bite leaves me violently ill for a few days. Then there are a range of insects that excrete acid as a defence mechanism. If this comes into contact with your skin, a painful acid burn will develop, which gets gradually worse over a few days. I have had the pleasure of this experience more times than I care to remember. All in all, it is rare for me not to have a bite or a sting or a burn on my arms or legs at any point in time.

Sometimes it's not even the animal's defence mechanism that causes me harm. I once sat with a stingless bee in my ear for an hour during a lecture that I was too shy to interrupt. By the end of the class, the bee had severely scratched my ear drum in a frantic attempt to find a way out of my ear canal. My ear became infected and I had to use antibiotic ear drops for a week to clear it up.

Surprisingly, birds and small mammals can be equally hazardous. I have lost count how many times birds and bats, misjudging the space above me, have flown into my head. My brother suggests it's because my hair looks like a bird's nest – I can't deny there could be some truth in that. But once, a bat not only hit me, but flew right into my mouth. I was running to catch up with a friend, when I opened my mouth to call out their name and a bat promptly flew in. The memory of its furry body on my tongue and the velvety soft wings slapping me in face still makes me squirm. I had to drink a lot of whiskey that night to wash away the remnants of bat. This amused my friends and family greatly, they have always said I have a big mouth – so big that a bat might mistake it for a cave, apparently.

These types of encounters are not conscious attacks, and as such, I just accept them as part of living in the bush. They are just creatures going about their business, without regard for who or what I am. There are two animals, however, that seem to undertake deliberate, intentional attacks on my belongings and my person - monkeys and squirrels. I know what you're thinking. How can anyone hate monkeys and squirrels? Well, don't let their fuzzy faces fool you. They are terrorists and I am at war with them.

I used to think they were cute, too. The first time I encountered a monkey was on that very first safari in Kenya. I hadn't closed my tent flaps properly, so when I returned from the morning safari, I found a monkey sitting on my bed reading a magazine. I am anthropomorphising a bit there. It wasn't quite reading the magazine - just looking at the pictures. I thought it was brilliant. *What fun, living alongside monkeys.* That was until I actually lived alongside monkeys.

If you live in a neighbourhood with monkeys, you will experience continuous break-ins. You cannot leave a window, a door, or a tent flap, as is usually my case, even remotely ajar. Turn your back for one second and the little ninjas will be inside before you know it.

Most often, they are in search of food. I wouldn't actually mind sharing the odd banana with them, if they asked nicely. But, they don't. They stage raids of the most destructive kind. First, they will send a decoy. One particularly attention-grabbing individual that will come perform a show for you on one side of the house. As you go to shoo it away, the rest of the mob will sneak in round the back. You only realise there has been a home invasion when you see the rest of the gang join the decoy, waving their loot in your face. If they took a couple of pieces of fruit, it'd be fine. But, you often return to the kitchen to find they have taken a bite out of every single piece of fruit in the bowl, leaving behind the discarded remains. *Why not take one whole banana, rather than one bite out of each of the bananas?* It's infuriating.

The raids are clearly premeditated. The timing is always too perfect to be purely coincidental. I suspect they have the house under surveillance. Usually, I'll have just finished making a sandwich when the decoy monkey appears on my verandah. Of course, after chasing him away, his co-conspirator has gone through the back door, stolen the sandwich, and left me with nothing but a plate of crumbs.

It's not always food. Sometimes it seems like they are just breaking in to have a jolly. When I was on my work experience placement, the tent I lived in was particularly susceptible to monkey raids. The front flaps didn't close and the rear of the tent opened out into an open-air bathroom with walls made of loosely stacked wooden poles. There was no way to keep the monkeys out. I never kept food in the tent, but every day when I came home from the field, it would look like there'd been a frat party inside. Despite the fact that I always made my bed before leaving for work, I'd come home to a crumpled mess. The bedding tossed around like there had been a pillow fight. The floor was strewn with toilet paper, books and anything else I might have left out of the cupboard by mistake. But the biggest mess was always in the bathroom. From what I could tell, the monkeys used the toilet as a water fountain, the shower as a toilet, and the sink as an art studio, smearing their faeces all over the basin and mirror. I quickly learnt to put my toothbrush away in the cupboard every day – I dread to think what they might have done with it otherwise.

I tried all sorts of measures to deter the monkeys including hanging rubber snakes around the tent. I even built a life-size James Bond scarecrow with a Sean Connery face mask that had been part of someone's fancy dress costume the previous month. None of it worked. If James Bond couldn't protect me from the monkey attacks nothing could. I had to resign myself to it being a reality of life in camp.

A few months after I had arrived at this camp, I started to get stomach cramps. Over the next couple of weeks, the cramps worsened and I was decidedly unwell. I volunteered to do the next supply run to town and made an appointment with the doctor.

I was explaining my symptoms to the doctor when my phone rang. It was my colleague back at camp.

"Hi, Rosie. I think I might know why you're sick."

"Ok, and...?"

"Tell the doctor you drank a dead monkey."

"I'm sorry, what?"

"I just found a monkey drowned in the water tank. Think it's been there some time."

I looked at the doctor, "Did you just hear that?"

It may have just been my imagination, but I was sure his face had turned a shade greener. "Yes. You're going to need a course of broad-spectrum antibiotics." He started to scrawl out a prescription.

As much as I hated the mess the monkeys made in my tent, I would never wish one of them harm, especially not to drown as a result of human activity in their habitat. It had been a particularly dry winter, so I presume the monkeys were desperate for some water. Maybe my rubber snake on the toilet seat had worked better than I realised and they had avoided drinking from my toilet one day and instead tried to reach the water in the tank. This one must have fallen in and, unable to reach the opening at the top from the water level, eventually drowned.

The task of extracting the monkey from the tank was horrendous. The monkey was ghostly white, colour had all but drained from the flesh, and its skin had become thin and translucent. One of my colleagues eventually managed to hook it with a snake stick. But, the body was already decomposing and the skin slipped right off the bones. The bulk of the carcass was eventually scooped out, but the skin and fur remained in the water, floating in a million pieces. The only option was to drain the tank and flush the flesh out.

It took multiple cycles of emptying and refilling the tank to wash all the pieces out. Once we were satisfied that the majority of the solid matter was out, we filled the tank with chlorine to disinfect it. This we then had to flush through the entire pipe network. I think we were overzealous with the chlorine, using enough to clean an Olympic size swimming pool. The water smelt of chlorine for weeks afterwards. Every time I washed my hair, I was afraid I was going to come out with bleached white locks.

It took about six months and three courses of antibiotics to fix my stomach. My sympathy for the monkeys had worn off long before my insides returned to normal. And while they avoided camp for a few weeks after the drowning incident, they soon returned to reign terror over me and my tent again.

Sadly, the monkey wasn't the only drowning incident in that camp. While my rubber snake had had limited success in deterring the monkeys from drinking from my toilet, it did scare a squirrel so much that it fainted, fell into the bowl and drowned.

At the time, I was pretty upset. I had never had any issues with squirrels up until that point. But that was soon to change.

While the squirrels didn't host raves in my tent like the monkeys, they did have other annoying habits. One particularly annoying trick they played was in the kitchen. There, they learnt to open the jar of peanut butter, eat their fill, then turn around and defecate into the jar, only to put the lid back on. The next person to come along craving peanut butter on toast was met with a disappointing jar of droppings.

Squirrels are also incessantly noisy creatures. On the one hand, it's great for alerting you to danger, especially snakes. On the other hand, they alarm-call at people, and will do so nonstop for hours until you move off again. Their alarm-call is high-pitched and squeaky. It sounds like someone giggling at you in an excessively mocking way. This is particularly annoying if you are trying to enjoy a peaceful afternoon in the garden. It is even worse if you are trying to sneak up on something exciting like a leopard. If squirrels are around, sneaking isn't possible. They will be sure to let every creature within earshot know there's a dangerous human predator on the prowl.

Squirrels also have an infuriating habit of chewing through cables, wires and pipes in the engine bay of my car. More than once, I've had to take my car for repairs after the squirrels have had their way. Once, it was particularly costly. I was driving along the highway when the temperature gauge on my dashboard shot up, there was a gurgling sound from the radiator, then steam started pouring out from under the bonnet. I pulled over on the side of the road to peer under the hood. I could see the radiator was boiling over, but I also noticed steam coming out at various points along the radiator hose. On closer inspection, I saw there were five or six holes along the hose with distinctive, rodent-shaped nibble marks. The squirrels had chewed through my radiator hose, causing it to leak and the engine to overheat. I knew I couldn't drive the vehicle, so I called a friend for help. They towed my vehicle to the mechanic who, by now, was used to me turning up with squirrel-induced damage.

I was car-less for weeks, not to mention my wallet was significantly lighter after the repairs. Ever since, I have parked my car with the bonnet up and a rubber snake placed somewhere in the engine bay. I laughed the first time I saw my colleague doing this, but I wish I had heeded their warning earlier and saved myself a few pennies. Now, if you see a car in the bush parked with the bonnet raised, you know why.

"I was safe in this world.
This was a place for creatures – I felt I had become
more of a creature than a girl.
I could handle myself in the wild."
- Aspen Matis[8]

Chapter 7

Misadventures of the Meat-Eating Kind

```
TEXT RECEIVED [28:12:2013, 20:17:42]
ROSIE: Hi Mum. Almost got eaten while wading
through the river today... but it wasn't a
crocodile or a hippo...
```

Being a big cat enthusiast, most of my research work has involved carnivores. Inevitably, I have had more than my fair share of close encounters with animals of the meat-eating kind. There was a running joke amongst my colleagues that if you can't find the lion or leopard you are looking for, just ask Rosie to go for a bush wee. That almost guarantees that the very animal you are looking for will appear, as if by magic, literally catching me with my pants down.

In my experience, carnivores either do exactly as you predict, making you look like Dr. Dolittle, or the precise opposite. I love when it is the former; it can be infuriating when it is the latter.

Whenever new volunteers arrived at the research project I was managing, the first thing they would have to endure was a tedious but important safety briefing from me. Some of these people had been travelling for over 24 hours and were understandably exhausted. I was used to seeing eyes glaze over as I tried to drive home the fact they were now in the middle of a reserve full of wild animals that might want to eat them. The house was not fenced so wild animals were very frequent visitors and the volunteers did not yet have the knowledge of how to keep themselves safe. It was critically important they follow my precise instructions on that first night, before their training began the next day.

One night, I had gathered the new volunteers on the verandah and I was giving my standard speech.

"Hyenas are the most frequent visitors," I explained, "so do not walk around outside at night. Do not leave your shoes outside at night, the hyenas will take them, it doesn't matter how smelly your feet are."

I was making eye contact with each individual to ensure they were paying attention.

"The last person to bed must close and lock the doors, otherwise the hyenas will come into the kitchen and raid the bins," I continued.

Instead of the usual glazed eyes I was used to, I was looking at a row of faces with eyes wide open. *Ah, for once they are actually paying attention,* I thought to myself.

"Yes, I know. It is hard to believe, but hyenas have come in and raided our bins many times before. You don't want to bump into one when you get up for a pee in the night."

Now, the row of faces was smirking, and this irritated me. *This is no laughing matter.* I was about to chide them for not taking the warning seriously, when one older lady piped up.

"Um… Rosie. There's a hyena behind you."

I spun round and standing in the open doorway behind me was a hyena, already halfway onto the verandah. It had a look on its face as if to say, "Who me?" Talk about perfect timing. Suffice to say, that group of volunteers were particularly good at closing the doors at night.

There is nothing more satisfying than being able to accurately predict animal behaviour. When gut instinct takes you straight to the animals you are looking for, the look of admiration from your passengers is priceless. However, when the animals do the opposite of what you expect, it can be exasperating.

I once spent a whole week searching for a particular male leopard we were researching. From our beds every night, we would hear him calling, but as I headed out at first light to track him down it was as if he had evaporated into thin air. I followed his tracks for hours each morning but never seemed to be able to catch up with him. The volunteers were starting to question my ability to track the leopard, and my stubbornness was kicking in - making me increasingly persistent in looking and increasingly short-tempered with anyone that questioned whether I would succeed.

After another fruitless morning, we headed back to camp for lunch. Carnivore research is nearly always done early in the morning and, then again, late afternoon to evening. In the heat of the day, the predators are less active, preferring to snooze in a shady spot until it cools down again.

As the volunteers tucked into their lunch, I could hear them moaning to the other group that we had failed to find the leopard again. I walked away, feeling the stroppiness boiling up inside me. From experience, I knew it was better to get away on my own for a bit, before I took out my frustrations on someone else. I could hear that the water tanks were overflowing, so I hopped back in the truck to go turn off the pump.

The water pump was a short drive away from camp along the river. I hadn't even made it out the driveway before I bumped into the leopard I had been looking for all week. Not only was he standing in plain sight in the open road, but he was hunting. *So much for predators not being active in the heat of the day.*

I watched him flush out a family of warthogs who were resting under a bush. One of the piglets escaped under my truck while the mother warthog squealed loudly and ran around in circles in an attempt to distract the leopard away from her other two scattering piglets. It was in vain. The piglets were so small, in two bounds the leopard was on them and all it took was a bat with a paw to dispatch them both. Realising all was lost the mother ran off, hopefully to reunite with her remaining piglet. The leopard picked up his catch - barely a snack for such a large leopard - and melted into the bushes.

Eager to brag to everyone back at the house that I not only saw the elusive leopard but witnessed him make a kill, I grabbed the radio to call it in.

"Base, this is Rosie. Guess who I just bumped into the driveway? Mr Leopard. He killed two warthogs."

"Do you have photographic evidence?" the radio crackled back.

"Um, no."

"If you can't prove it, it never happened."

They were only winding me up, but they had a point. I wouldn't have believed it if I hadn't seen it with my own eyes. Determined to get some evidence, I followed the leopard into the bushes and managed to snap one grainy photo on my phone. You could barely tell it even was a leopard. But it was enough to convince the others. I swore to myself that from then on I would take my camera everywhere, even if it was just to turn the water pump off.

Lions are even worse than leopards for not behaving as the textbooks describe. Two examples of this particularly come to mind, both involving the same male lion.

Within fenced reserves, the animals have limited opportunities to disperse and meet mates they aren't closely related to, so interventions are sometimes required. This reserve had just received two new lionesses from another part of the country, brought in to diversify the gene pool in the lion population. When new animals arrive, they are held in an enclosure, called a boma, for a while, to acclimatise to their new surroundings. It also allows us to monitor their health and condition before release. The holding bomas are located inside the reserve so other animals are able to see, but not have physical contact with, the new arrivals.

For the two months that these new females were in the boma, this particular male lion barely left their side. He sat, day and night, outside their boma keeping guard over them, adamant that they would belong to him and no one else. I don't blame him, they were stunning specimens. But when the time came to let the girls out, we were worried the male might be overly amorous with them. We wanted the girls to have the chance to come out the boma in their own time. The male had recently received a kick to the face from a zebra and had a broken tooth as a result. The vet was keen to take a look at the damage, so we darted the lion and took him to another holding boma on the other side of the reserve. This provided the perfect opportunity to let the girls out with some breathing space from their over-eager suitor.

The day of the release came and the excitement was palpable. I sent one team to the girls' boma, to open their gate and record their activity in the following hours. I took another group to the male's boma. Once I received confirmation from the other team that the girls had left their boma, I opened his gate to let him out.

"This is going to be interesting," I said to my team. "This guy is going to hoof it back to his girls, but I don't know what the reunion is going to be like. I suspect these girls are going to be more then he bargains for."

As soon as I opened the gate, he came trotting out and made a beeline for the other boma. We struggled to keep up with him, as he followed a straight path through the bush, while I had to stick to the roads. I was doing a good job of predicting where he would emerge from each block, regularly glimpsing him as he marched along.

We reached a point where I knew there was a dry riverbed up ahead after which the road split in two entirely different directions. I wanted to get ahead of him, so I would be in a good position to see which route he took as he emerged from the river crossing. I could see him on my right, just about to reach the river, so I sped up to pass through the riverbed. We parked on the other side and waited for him to appear.

We waited and waited. He never emerged.

"Shit! How did we lose him?" I said. I played various scenarios in my head. Could he have backtracked, or did he walk along the river. Neither seemed logical to me. *He was heading straight for the girls. Why would he suddenly change course?*

I drove back to the riverbed and then along it to find his tracks in the sand. I picked them up where we had last seen him about to drop into the riverbed. We followed them and found he had, in fact, turned and gone along the riverbed. I couldn't understand why, unless it was the placement of my truck that had put him off. This seemed unlikely as he was so habituated to vehicles; he had never run from them before.

We rounded a bend in the riverbed and were suddenly struck by what had distracted him from his mission to find love. Food! He was busy tucking into a zebra carcass. I could tell he hadn't it killed himself. Apart from the fact that there hadn't been time and we would have heard the commotion, I could see the zebra had been dead at least a few hours and was already partially eaten. I suspected it was a leopard kill that the lion had happened across. It turns out that if there's one thing more enticing than sex to a male, it's food.

The lion sat and gorged himself for two days. Then, inexplicably killed another zebra less than ten metres away, gorging on that for another three days. It was as if he had forgotten all about his lady friends. Or, maybe, after months of sitting by their side and not eating properly, he was feeling skinny and wanted to bulk up a bit for them - make a good impression. On the fifth night, while we were all tucked up asleep in bed, having given up on the excitement of the reunion, he eventually went to go find the girls. We will never know what the first contact was like, but by morning all was serene and a new pride had been formed.

This same male lion surprised us on another occasion.

A friend of mine was undertaking a practical assessment as part of his qualifications to take guests on walking safaris, armed with a rifle. The assessment required him to guide some proxy guests into a sighting with a dangerous animal, and safely get them out again, all the while being observed by an assessor. I, along with another colleague, volunteered to be his guests. Another friend of ours was coming as a back-up rifle carrier.

We headed to where this particular male lion had been seen earlier in the day, at one of his favourite dams. We pulled up just short of the dam and hopped out the truck. For the assessment to be valid, we weren't allowed to find the animal from the truck first, it had to be tracked on foot. The two guys prepared their rifles, while the assessor explained how the assessment would work. From that point onwards, everything was considered part of the assessment and we had to pretend to be real guests. We were to follow instructions provided by the lead rifle handler. If things went sideways, we were to listen to the assessor only. We had to feign ignorance of any bush knowledge ourselves.

The guy being assessed started with his safety briefing. It was deadly serious, but because we were all such close friends, we got the nervous giggles. Not wanting to ruin his assessment, I tried to keep a straight face and acknowledge the fact that we were actually doing something potentially dangerous. Despite knowing this lion since birth, we rarely had any interactions with him on foot - except on the occasions he had interrupted me bush-weeing. We didn't really know how he was going to react to the sight of five humans walking towards him. We also had no idea whether he was alone, if he had a kill, or if there were any other factors that could influence how the animal would react.

It was now late morning and the heat was rising. We had a good hunch that the lion would no longer be sitting in the sun by the water. There was a shady drainage line that ran along the northern end of the dam and we guessed he might be lying up in there. It was thick bush - exactly where you don't really want to bump into a lion as you would most likely be on top of him before you even saw him.

Walking along the dam wall, we picked up his tracks and, as predicted, they were heading into the drainage line. Rather than follow them straight down through the thickest part of the bush, our guide made the sensible decision to head back along the dam wall and enter the drainage line where the road cut across it. The vegetation was more open there so it would afford us better visibility. We walked, in single file, up the drainage line. In the deep sand, the walking was slow going and took effort, but without vegetation underfoot we were able to move quietly. As the drainage line narrowed, the bushes closed in around us. It was like walking through a tunnel. With the two rifle holders ahead of me, I had limited visibility of what lay in front. I had to follow blindly as a real guest would. *I really hope they are paying attention,* I thought to myself.

The tension grew as we moved further into the vegetation. I felt like I was on a rollercoaster waiting for the big drop - there was the anticipation that something scary was about to happen, but I wasn't in control of what or when. The difference being, on a rollercoaster, while it is scary to plummet at great speed, you are pretty confident nothing bad is going to happen. Bumping into a male lion, weighing around 280kg and housing a fearsome set of teeth and claws, didn't offer the same assurance.

Given that I couldn't see ahead of me, I started letting my eyes wander from side to side, picking out trees that I might be able to climb if things didn't go to plan. I couldn't see many and, if you recall, I am really bad at climbing trees anyway. As this thought was passing through my head, I saw the hand of the guy at the front go up, open handed, palm facing forwards - the silent signal to stop. Obediently I froze, leaving one foot still dangling in the air.

The guy turned and whispered, "He's right up ahead, sleeping under that date palm. Do you see?"

I peered round his shoulder, almost losing my balance before realising I could put my hanging foot down to stop myself from falling over. About 50 metres ahead of us sat the unmistakable tawny mound of a lion.

"I think we can get a little closer," he continued. The assessor nodded in agreement. I started doing the sums in my head about charging speeds of lion. Fifty metres away meant we had just over two seconds to respond. *Can I reach and climb that tree in two seconds? Seems unlikely.*

We inched, slowly and quietly, closer to the sleeping lion. Of course, this lion was not fully asleep. As usual with wild animals, the ears were still actively listening for any danger. Even the lion king has to be permanently on guard. After we gained another ten metres, he let it be known that he was perfectly aware we were sneaking up on him. He opened one eye, lifted his head a few centimetres and gave us a piercing look. We froze. I mapped my escape route in my head, all the while watching and waiting to see what he would do next.

He simply lowered his head and went back to sleep.

We stood in silence for a few minutes, not really believing our eyes and wondering whether it was a ruse. Was he actually going to leap up and charge ferociously towards us?

He remained in repose. Eventually, our guide signalled for us to back off and we made our way back the way we came in silence.

Only once we reached the car did someone speak. It was the assessor.

"I am not sure I can sign you off for that. Either that lion was drugged, or he is someone's pet. I have never, in all my decades of doing this, seen less of a reaction from a lion."

We burst out laughing. The tension of the last hour released in floods through our bodies. I can't speak for the guy being assessed, because I am sure I would have felt differently being in his shoes, but I did feel a little disappointed we hadn't seen more of a reaction. Sometimes it's good to have a little scare.

As the saying goes, you should be careful what you wish for. Because I got my scare a few months later – this time by a leopard, and this time it was entirely unanticipated.

Christmas was the only time of the year we didn't have volunteers at the project. Whilst this gave the chance for most the staff to take leave and visit families, someone had to stay back to continue the research. I always volunteered to stay on as I loved the opportunity to spend hours in the bush on my own without the burden of satisfying anyone else's needs.

On one such Christmas break, some friends staying nearby called to ask if they could come on drive with me that afternoon. Given they were only visiting for one drive, I felt under pressure to show them a few good sightings. Despite the fact that lions are my least favourite of the predators, they are always a winner with visitors and relatively easy to find. Furthermore, one of the ladies had never seen a lion in the wild before, so it would be rude for me not to try.

One of the lions in the group had a radio tracker, allowing us to locate her using radio telemetry. After driving to the area where they had last been seen, I climbed up on the roof of the truck and listened for any beeps from my radio receiver that would give me an indication of their location. Radio silence.

I kept driving, stopping every kilometre or so to check again. Still, nothing. I was getting frustrated. *Where could they have gone? The lions are supposed to be easy.*

Just as I was about to give up hope, I thought I heard something. I wasn't certain, because when you have been listening too hard for too long you do have a tendency to start hearing what we call phantom beeps, but I was getting desperate.

"That could have been something," I said noncommittally. "Should we carry on and check it out?"

"Oooh, yes please," they replied enthusiastically.

If it was a beep, it was coming from the other side of the river. It had recently rained heavily, and the river was in full flow. If I had been on my own, I wouldn't have bothered, but feeling under pressure to find the lion for my guests, I followed the only lead I had.

I drove along the road to the next river crossing. Parking at the top of the riverbank above the crossing, I leapt out the car, "Wait here. I am going to walk down to see whether the river is crossable. I haven't been across since the last rain and it is looking quite deep."

I set off down the steep, slippery bank. Having gone about ten metres, I paused and shouted over my shoulder, "Whatever you do, don't get out of the vehicle. This is prime leopard habitat!"

They stuck their thumbs up in acknowledgement, and I continued down to the water's edge. From the tracks in the mud, I could see no one had crossed the river at this point since the last rains, but seeing the flow up close, it didn't seem too strong. I was satisfied that we wouldn't be pushed downstream by the force of the water. What I couldn't tell was whether the action of the floods had made deep holes in the soft river sand under the water which might cause us to get stuck. If in doubt, it is always better to walk the crossing first and check. So I did.

I cautiously stepped one foot into the river. The cool water felt refreshing on what was a hot and sticky day. The ground was fairly solid, so I brought my other foot in. Step by step, I edged my way through the water. At first, it was only ankle deep, so I wasn't too afraid of hippo or crocodile. But the water crept higher as I came to the middle of the river. Eventually, the water was above my knees, the occasional wave splashing the bottom of my shorts. With the water at this depth, I was focused on not losing my footing. I didn't feel like having a river bath and spending the rest of the drive in wet clothes. I was also now scanning the water on either side, keeping an eye out for any ripples or bubbles that might give away an approaching underwater crocodile.

This meant I wasn't concentrating on what was ahead of me, so I was startled when I heard a crash in the bushes on the opposite bank. Before I lifted my gaze, I assumed I had disturbed a bushbuck – a small, shy antelope often found along the edges of rivers. When I did focus my eyes on the bank opposite me, I saw something far less benign.

Tearing down the bank towards me was a huge, male leopard. The deep throated growling cut right through my chest like a knife. Without thinking, I threw my arms up into the air.

"You motherf*****!!!"

I didn't even recognise it as my own voice. It sounded deep and menacing, very unlike me. I continued to wave my arms above my head making myself look as big as possible. When the leopard reached the water's edge, it paused and looked me straight in the eyes. *Go on, turn around. You don't want to come in this water,* I urged the leopard telepathically. Having experienced the leopard in the swimming pool years before, I knew the cats could swim, but I assumed he would be reluctant to do so. I kicked my legs and splashed water toward him, trying to highlight the fact that he was going to have to swim to reach me. I shouted again, "Go! Go! You f*****"

Thankfully, this was enough to make the leopard think twice. He turned around and slunk, belly low to the ground, back into the bushes a few metres up the bank. That's as far as he was prepared to back off though. I could see the white tip of his tail flicking agitatedly within the bushes. I knew I couldn't turn my back or he might take his chance with me. So I made the painstaking journey to my side of the bank - inch by inch - backwards.

My arms were still held aloft as I talked to the leopard, "Ok, I am going. I am sorry I disturbed you. But don't come after me, you hear me?"

After what felt like an eternity, I eventually felt the bank behind my heels. I negotiated stepping back up onto the solid ground with my eyes still fixed on the white tail tip going *flick, flick, flick.* No longer impeded by the water, I could move much faster, though still backwards, not willing to risk turning my back to the leopard.

Nearing the top of the bank, I heard a call from the truck.

"Rosie, are you ok? What the hell happened? We could hear you shouting."

I yelled back, "Yeah, all good. Just had a run in with a leopard." I turned and gave them a wink to reassure them I was fine.

Confident I was now a safe distance from the leopard, I jogged the final few metres back to the truck.

"So, yeah, nearly got eaten by a leopard. But the crossing is fine, so let's go. He's still sitting there so you might get a glimpse."

I negotiated the truck down the steep bank and through the crossing with ease, there were no holes to get stuck in even beyond the point I had reached before my encounter with the leopard. The ascent on the opposite bank was challenging though. I hadn't noticed the sheer drop from the bank into the water on this side, having been distracted by the leopard. I made a mental note to myself that coming back this way was potentially risky with the chance that the front wheels would sink into the river sand coming off the drop.

Once on the other bank, the leopard was nowhere to be seen. He had likely taken the opportunity to slip away while I was negotiating the ascent out of the river. Annoyingly, the lions were nowhere to be found either. We drove around for another hour and didn't pick up any more beeps. I had to admit the phantom beep we had on the other side of the river had been a false alarm. It was time to head back south. Wanting to avoid getting stuck in the crossing, I decided to drive an extra half an hour along the river to cross further down.

This time, I opted to take the plunge without checking the state of the sand below. The charge from the leopard was exhilarating, but I would rather not bump into anything else today. Needless to say, we got halfway across the river and fell into a hole. We were stuck and no amount of manoeuvring could get us out. I tried to radio for assistance, but the river banks blocked any signal. *Looks like I am bloody wading again*, I thought.

I grabbed my handheld radio and turned to my passengers.

"Stay put, again. Sorry! I am just going to walk up to the top of the bank to get a signal to radio for help."

I couldn't open my door because the river was flowing hard against it. I climbed out my window, crawled along the bonnet and then lowered myself into the water holding the radio above my head. The water here was much deeper and my shorts were instantly soaked. Making a conscious decision not to worry about what animals I might bump into, I pushed through the water and legged it up the bank.

A nearby lodge responded to my plea for help and soon had us pulled free – minus a wing mirror that was swiped off in the process.

'Ok, no more river crossings," I said to my passengers. "Let's go look for the cheetah instead."

A puddle was forming on my seat from my drenched shorts, but I was smiling to myself all the same. *I handled a full-blown leopard charge like a pro today.* It was immensely empowering.

> *"She was wild and free with a dab*
> *of logic in between,*
> *chasing her dreams and following*
> *her heart beat."*
>
> *- Nikki Rowe*[9]

Chapter 8

Misadventures of the Giant, Grey Kind

```
TEXT RECEIVED [11:08:2013, 19:13:09]
ROSIE:   Hi  Mum.  The  house  was  burgled  this
afternoon.  The  thieves  were  three  metres  tall
and weighed approximately five tonnes...
```

Despite a shaky start with elephants, I actually learnt to love them. They are certainly an animal to be revered and respected - they can flip a car like you or I could flip an Ikea coffee table. However, they possess an intelligence and a sense of humour that allows for interactions on a different level to those with other animals.

People always look at me as if I am mad when I say elephants are funny. Trust me, they are both smarter and funnier than many people I know. I can demonstrate this by sharing some stories about a couple of bull elephants I got to know particularly well.

It is pretty standard practice that, once tired of your company, elephants will put large logs, and even entire trees, in the middle of the road as you approach. They will then swagger down the road with you now unable to follow, throwing you a sideways glance just to make sure you know it was entirely intentional. These specific bulls, though, would play games with me on a whole different level.

If there is one fruit elephant go crazy for, it is the marula fruit. This fruit resembles a golf ball in both size and hardness. More like a sour gobstopper than a fruit, there is very little flesh around the hard stone in the centre. Eating one involves sucking the flesh until it has lost its flavour. It is, however, packed with vitamin C and is highly nutritious. It can be made into jams and jellies, as well as homebrew beer. Perhaps, most famously, it is the key ingredient in Amarula, the African fruity equivalent of Baileys liqueur. When in season, at the height of summer, female marula trees grow heavy with a glut of these fruits, and fructivorous animals travel from far and wide to take advantage of the bounty. None more so than the elephant.

My unfenced garden was blessed with many large and bountiful marula trees. For a few weeks during the fruiting season, it was a treacherous activity to walk across the driveway - the ground became a carpet of golf ball-like fruits and twisted ankles were a common result. The elephants only compounded this issue.

I have an uncanny knack of being able to sleep through almost any human-induced noise. I can happily dream the night away while a party, with music and frivolities aplenty, rages outside my bedroom door. The tiniest noise from an animal, however, and I am wide awake. I will rouse to a leopard calling two kilometres away, or the delicate nibble of an impala outside my window. I don't want to miss any opportunity to experience nature, especially not at night when all the wild things come out to play. But, when the elephants raid the marula trees, even the deepest sleeper won't be able to sleep through it.

While the rest of the herd politely targets the trees on the periphery of the garden, these two bulls would turn their attention to the marula trees in the driveway. This is how it would normally play out.

Thunk, putt, putt, putt. Thunk, putt, putt, putt.

There's no easing into it. You are rudely awakened by the jolting *thunk* of one of these marula fruits bouncing off the corrugated tin roof above your head, quickly followed by several more. The elephants shake the branches to make the fruits fall. Once satisfied that they've made enough noise, they move on to the trees under which we park the cars.

Thunk, putt, putt, putt. Thunk, putt, putt, putt. Crash. Screech.

This time, entire branches are brought down, right on the car roof and dragged down the windscreen. Car insurance companies in South Africa send you text message warnings when hailstones are expected, to allow you to park your car somewhere it won't get damaged. There's no such alert for elephants with marula fruit projectiles, which are equally, if not more, damaging.

It is usually at this point that I haul myself out of bed and venture to the doorway with a torch issuing my first caution.

"Hey! Stop that Mister! Why can't you just eat the ones already on the floor like the rest of us do?"

That's when I get the sideways glance, which can only mean one thing - they are not done playing games. Never satisfied with the branches and fruit they have brought down already, the elephants eye the one particular branch with the best-looking fruit. That's when they squeeze their five-tonne bulk between two of the cars, leaning against them to get a leg up. They stand on their hind legs straining to reach that one special branch. I watch as the car starts to tip on an angle.

"Hey! No! Stop that!" I scream, now running out into the driveway in my pyjamas, flashing the torch in their faces. It's completely in vain. They won't move on until they are satisfied that they've won the game. It amuses the volunteers though, who by now are peering out the windows from the safety of their bunk beds, giggling at the sight of their very serious manager running around in bare feet and PJs, dwarfed by the great elephant silhouettes in the torchlight.

In the morning, the full extent of the game is revealed. Branches and fruit strewn everywhere. It takes a good half hour to clear up the mess before the vehicles can leave for work.

1-0 to the elephants.

In winter, the elephants visit the garden for a different reason - water.

Winter in the lowveld is the dry season. The rivers are parched channels of sand and many of the smaller pans become arid dust bowls. Larger waterholes retain some water, but it quickly becomes stagnant and murky. While most animals will make do, elephant are notoriously fussy drinkers and will go out of their way to find fresh, clean water. The easiest place to find that is where the humans live.

Our water supply came from a borehole about one kilometre from the house. The water was pumped through pipes running along the ground to a large water tank just uphill of the house. The water was then gravity-fed to the building. While the water tank was relatively well protected, sitting inside a large round concrete dam, the pipes were unavoidably vulnerable to elephant attack.

At the driest times of the year, the elephants would break the pipes on a daily basis. If they broke the pipes close to the house and during the day, it would normally be witnessed and repairs could be made quickly before the entire 15,000 litre storage tank was drained. If they did it under the cover of darkness, or somewhere along the pipeline from the borehole, we often wouldn't notice until we were completely out of water and left with an airlock in the system. I became highly proficient in plumbing repairs. But I also grew weary of not being able to wash my hair at least once a week.

On one occasion, the elephants broke the pipes while I was in the shower, the water running out just as I had a full lather of shampoo in my hair. Wiping the suds out of my eyes with a towel, I threw on some clothes, grabbed my car keys and stormed out of the house, screaming profanities at the top of my voice. Without explanation to anyone, I drove off, spitting up gravel as I went. I drove the hour and a half journey to our neighbours' house, interrupting a dinner they were having with friends. I apologised for the intrusion but begged to wash the shampoo out my hair and then I would be on my way. I can only imagine what a bizarre sight I must have been, sodden and soapy. But people in the bush are pretty unflappable to strange events like that.

2–0 to the elephants.

That was the only time I really got angry at the elephants. Most of the time, I found it amusing rather than annoying. Even when they were clearly playing games with us.

Just outside the front door of the house was a garden tap to which we attached a hosepipe to wash down the cars. One lunchtime, when everyone was back at the house, one of the volunteers alerted us to the presence of an elephant by the tap. The entire household headed to the front door or sat at the windows to marvel at this giant beast standing only a few metres from the house. Cameras were clicking and the volunteers were engrossed in this exciting opportunity to be so close to an elephant outside of a vehicle.

My colleagues and I were not as excited because we knew he was up to something. He had one front foot resting on top of the garden tap, light as a feather. He eyed us with that sideways look and once satisfied a suitably large audience was watching, he pressed down onto the tap.

"Don't you dare, Mister!" my colleague next to me shouted.

The elephant paused, teasingly, for a second, before continuing to weigh down on the tap. It buckled under his weight and eventually it snapped straight off, water gushing into the air. Using his trunk, he sucked up a few litres of the liquid and squirted it into his mouth. The second trunkful he sprayed over his head as if celebrating his own hilarious joke. Then, he tossed his head and sauntered off. A broken tap for one mouthful of water hardly seemed worth it. It clearly wasn't for hydration, it was for the joy of the game.

3–0 to the elephants.

If you are still not persuaded these elephants were playing games with me, perhaps this next story will convince you. Because, in this instance, there was nothing to gain for the elephant except pure pleasure.

The rest of the household was away on an excursion for a week. An intern and I had volunteered to stay back to continue the research work. One evening, we were arriving back at the house after a long afternoon in the field. I turned off the main road into the driveway and knew instantly that the elephants had paid us a visit while we were out. Every couple of metres, there was a tree pushed over into the road. It looked like a tornado had come through. The last 100 metres to the house took us a good five minutes to traverse as we navigated around, or got out and moved, the debris in order to pass. While hauling trees and branches off the road, it never occurred to me that the elephants were still at the house. So, when we moved the last obstacle and turned the final corner of the driveway, it came as quite a surprise when the entire herd hurtled past us.

What was even more surprising was that the elephants appeared to be doing some sort of a fancy-dress parade.

The first elephant was carrying something that looked like a bed sheet in its trunk, flailing it back and forth like a matador with a cape. The second elephant had a square of old carpet planted, like a mortar board, on top of its head and was strutting with its chin held high and proud. A flurry of younger elephant careered past in an excited hysteria. If they had props, they had dropped them, maybe nerves getting the better of them. But the last elephant, the naughtiest of the bulls, had no such self-confidence issues. He was the master of the games. He sauntered along holding a white plastic garden chair in his trunk, whipping it around in circles above his head like a school boy whipping his shirt around after scoring a goal in football. The scene was beyond hilarious, and we sat in the car with tears of laughter streaming down our cheeks.

The elephants had taken advantage of the rare empty house and had raided the open verandah for trophies to steal. I even began to wonder if the elephants had put all those obstacles in the driveway to slow our progress and warn them of our return, giving them enough time to make their escape. I wouldn't put it past them.

4–0 to the elephants.

You may not believe elephants are smart enough for such planning. But, I do.

This same group of elephants also had a habit of breaking out of the reserve, sometimes for no apparent reason other than to have a frolic on the road. They only ever broke out at night, under the cover of darkness, and by daybreak were always huddled together, seemingly innocent, right in the middle of the reserve again. When I would question them the next day about the less-than-subtle piles of elephant poo on the road outside, I always imagined them saying, "Who us? Couldn't possibly have been us. We have been here in the middle of the reserve all night."

The breaking out wasn't the smart bit, it was the way they would do it. The two naughty bulls were always the ringleaders. If they had convinced some younger, less-experienced but eager-to-impress bulls to join them, they would then take full advantage of them. They would use these innocent youngsters as battering rams and push them right through the electric fence, ensuring that it was the youngsters that took the full brunt of the voltage. If they were alone, and didn't fancy taking the shock themselves, they would head to one of the many gates and simply pick the lock.

It took us a while to work out this escape strategy. Several times, we found elephant debris on the road when we were coming home from the pub. After searching the entire fence line for the break that would have to be fixed in the morning, we found none. It was puzzling. When an elephant breaks a fence, it is pretty obvious. There is usually a gaping, elephant-sized hole in the fence, big enough to drive a car through. We couldn't find any such holes, but the elephants had clearly been out as their trail of destruction and mountains of poo were everywhere.

Eventually, we followed their tracks until we found the point at which they had gone in and out the fence. It led us straight to a gate. When we examined the gate, it was still intact. They hadn't broken the gate, so how did they get out? It was only on closer examination that we saw the padlock holding the gate closed had been forced open. Using their immensely strong but nimble trunks they must have levered the padlock, pushed open the gate, and had their playtime outside.

What is really remarkable, though, is that they then returned the same way, closing the gate behind them again. That's both smart and funny in my book.

5-0 to the elephants.

It wasn't all games and silliness with the elephant, though. Their high degree of social intelligence means they have a knack for 'reading the room' and I had several tender moments with them too. One of my favourites was when I was out at night in a lightning storm. The storm was still in the distance so there was no rain and I couldn't hear the thunder, but the night sky was illuminated every few seconds by flashes of lightning.

I had parked in a riverbed where the skyline was more open. With my engine and headlights off, I was enjoying nature's light show. There were a few minutes without a flash and I sat in complete darkness listening to the sound of the surrounding night only to find when the next flash came that I had been encircled by the elephants. True to form, they had approached in stealth mode and were peering at me from close range. Rather than playing tricks, I felt they had acknowledged my peaceful demeanour and hadn't wanted to disturb me. They continue to stand around in silent reverie for another ten minutes before quietly carrying on their way.

On my last day on the reserve, I sought out the elephant herd to say my goodbyes. It was heart-wrenching to leave, and as much as the elephants had driven me nuts, it was extremely emotional to know I may never see them again. As if sensing my mood, the elephants came out of the drainage line where they had been feeding and approached my car in single file. One-by-one they came to my door and looked me right in the eyes, some of them raising their trunk towards my face as if saluting me before quietly moving on. The procession took several minutes, and the lump in my throat grew bigger with each passing elephant.

As always, bringing up the rear was the naughtiest of the bulls. Despite all the pranks he had played on me over the years, saying goodbye to him was the hardest of all. Standing next to me, he raised his trunk. I whispered farewell, tempted to raise my hand to meet his trunk. But before sentimentality got the better of me, he used his trunk to knock the hat right off my head. A snigger erupted out my nose. *You just had to have the last laugh, didn't you?* It epitomised our relationship to a T, and I couldn't have asked for a better send off.

6-0 to the elephants.

> *"It's a terrifying thought,*
> *A Red-Riding Hood,*
> *Who knew exactly*
> *What she was doing*
> *When she invited the wild in."*
>
> *- Nikita Gill*[10]

Chapter 9

Misadventures of the Horny Kind

```
TEXT RECEIVED [23:09:2014, 19:03:12]
ROSIE: Hi Mum. I learnt how to climb trees
today. The trick is to get chased up one by
something with a very large and pointy horn...
```

Rhinos, the other grey giants of Africa, are not as smart as their elephant counterparts. But their simpleness is part of what makes them so endearing.

After being charged by the black rhino mother on my first drive, I have had few more encounters with them since. White rhino, though, continue to be a firm favourite of mine. They do relatively little apart from eat grass and sleep, but they have such a gentle calmness that I feel at peace whenever around them.

One group of rhinos perfectly summed this up for me - a trio of young adults, two males and a female. They were inseparable, always grazing within a few metres of each other and maintaining physical contact with each other when they slept. Despite being unrelated, their bond was extremely strong.

The young female was of breeding age, and her male friends were not suitable mates as they were subordinate to the big male who dominated the area. At some point, she must have snuck off and mated with the big bull while the boys weren't looking, as I noticed she was looking rather rotund and suspected she was pregnant.

One morning, I bumped into the two boys, but the female wasn't with them. Both were, as usual, heads to the ground grazing the grass like giant lawnmowers. However, once I got within earshot, I could hear, between the munching, both boys whimpering. It was the most unexpected sound to come from a two-tonne beast, child-like in pitch and tone. Every few minutes, one would lift his head and sniff loudly, before resuming the simultaneous sobbing and munching. They were crying. I could only assume crying because their best friend was missing. It was such a comical, yet touching, sight to see these enormous and powerful males blubbering like babies.

I wasn't worried about their friend, though. I suspected she left to go have her calf in peace, without these two lumbering babies getting in the way. And, I was right. The very next morning we found her with the tiniest calf, still wet with wobbly legs. We called him Little Nelson, in honour of the great Nelson Mandela, who had passed away that morning. It wasn't long before she introduced her baby to her two friends, and they seemed to get over their abandonment issues - the bond between the three friends remained strong.

If a fully-grown adult rhino crying is endearing and rather funny, a baby rhino crying is one of the most heart-breaking sounds on this planet. Not least because it is so often associated with the loss of their mother to poachers.

Just over a year after Little Nelson was born, poachers came onto the reserve and fired two shots. The alarm was raised and the anti-poaching team responded instantly, chasing the poachers out of the reserve. At first light, I joined the anti-poaching team in the search to find any injured rhinos. The first group I found were four youngsters, who had been in the area where the shots were fired the previous night, but were now over eight kilometres away. They were clearly distressed, huddled together and whimpering, seemingly too nervous to put their heads down to eat. I was certain they had been shot at, but apart from scratches running down their flanks, likely sustained when fleeing through thorny acacia bushes, they seemed to be unharmed. I stayed with them for a while, talking in a soft voice to make sure they were ok. I only left once they settled down and were nibbling on bits of grass.

My feeling of relief that the rhinos were unscathed was short-lived as I then got a call over the radio from a colleague who had been searching a different part of the reserve. He had found the trio of friends, and Little Nelson's mother was limping badly.

"She isn't putting any weight on her front left leg," he reported, "and I can see a trail of blood where she's been walking."

We called the vet and managed to dart her to take a closer look. Once she was down, her injuries were so shocking it took my breath away. She had been shot in the face, the bullet entering through her left eye. It then ricocheted off her cheek bone and rebounded into her leg. The eyeball was mush and her leg was floppy, possibly broken. Rhinos have poor eyesight anyway, so losing one eye would not have been such an issue. But an animal the size and weight of a rhino cannot survive on three legs. In a field environment, with a wild animal of that size, there was relatively little we could do with the broken leg. Putting a plaster cast on was not an option. However, wild animals are phenomenally resilient and the vet couldn't be sure of how bad the injury to the leg was, so it was decided to give her another 12 hours to see if there was any improvement.

I attached a spare radio collar to one good leg to keep track of her. Then, we drew up a roster to stay with her for the next 12 hours. There was a good chance that the poachers, having not succeeded in removing the prized horn, would be back to find the injured rhino. We set up a guard to protect her throughout the night.

The whole time we had been working on the female, the two males and her calf, Little Nelson, had been circling around making bleating noises. As soon as we backed off, the female got to her feet and they rushed back to her side to comfort her. Not wanting to distress them further, we waited just out of sight, but close enough that we could monitor their movements using the radio receiver linked to the collar on her leg. I took the first shift, during which time they barely moved.

At around midnight, I handed the radio receiver to a colleague and headed home for some rest. Unfortunately, sleep does not come easily when you are worried about an animal you care about deeply. Before daybreak, not remotely refreshed, I got up, grabbed a cup of tea and some toast to go, and headed back to the rhinos. I found the group a short distance away from where they had been the night before, but the two males and the calf were on top of a cliff overlooking the river, and the female was now down in the riverbed. There was no pathway down to the river at this point and, from the way she was now stumbling about, I could tell she had fallen down the cliff - a sheer drop of a few metres.

She was now in a worse state than she had been the night before. She could only manage a couple of shuffling steps before passing out and crashing face down into the sand. A process she repeated over and over again, making agonisingly slow progress across the riverbed. It was extremely difficult to watch.

I called the Reserve Manager with an update and a recommendation to euthanise her. After a discussion with the management team and reserve owners, it was agreed by all that her injuries were too severe and the kindest thing to do at this point was to end her suffering. I sat on the roof of my truck 100 metres away when the mercy shot was fired. The crack of the high calibre rifle smashed through my body like I had been hit by the bullet myself. A single tear rolled down my right cheek.

"I'm sorry, my girl," I whispered to her spirit. "I will take good care of your baby, I promise."

A crackle came over my radio, "She's down," the solemn voice confirmed.

There was no more time for self-indulgent sorrow. I wiped the tear from my cheek and snapped into auto-mode. I still had a job to do.

With the methodical precision of a crime scene investigation team, we set about removing her prized horns with a chainsaw, so they could be stored safely in an undisclosed location to prevent them getting into the wrong hands. We also dissected her leg to remove the bullet that would be given to the authorities as evidence. I was feeling a pang of guilt every few minutes. Maybe I had made the wrong call, and we could have saved her. But once we opened up her leg, we could see the bones had been shattered into pieces, I stopped counting after I had removed the twentieth shard. There was no chance to save the leg. We had made the right decision.

A short while later, the authorities arrived to take statements and bag the evidence. Once all the formalities were completed, I called the house and asked my colleagues to bring the volunteers to the scene. It may seem macabre, cruel even, especially given they had only arrived two days earlier. But these volunteers had come to South Africa to learn about real wildlife conservation and it doesn't get more real than a rhino shot by poachers paid to hack off its the horn.

I can only imagine what they must have thought of me. Normally, when new volunteers arrive, I spend their first few days in almost constant contact with them, introducing them to their new surroundings and making sure they settle in properly. This group, I had picked up from the airport and after their initial safety briefing - the one warning about hyena in the kitchen - I had gone to bed and then not seen them since. My hair is dishevelled at the best of times, but it was now severely frazzled, mirroring my nerves. Having not slept, I had large dark circles under my eyes and was now plastered with rhino blood. I must have looked like a crazed, wild woman that had been lost in the woods for the past ten years. I suspect the look of fear and horror on a lot of their faces had more to do with how I looked, than the rhino carcass laying prone behind me.

After describing the events that had taken place and giving an impromptu lecture on the devastating state of rhino poaching in South Africa - a lecture I should have given them in the classroom that morning - I sent them back to camp. I wasn't ready to go back, though. I needed to check on Little Nelson.

At 15-months-old, Little Nelson was weaned but still dependent on his mother for protection. Baby rhinos can easily fall prey to lions and hyenas if not protected by an adult. Now, I had to make the second hardest decision of the day - do we capture Little Nelson and take him to a rhino orphanage? Removing an animal from the wild is always a last resort. It is extremely difficult to rehabilitate most species back into the wild once they have been cared for in captivity. But, I knew he wouldn't survive on his own.

It didn't take me long to find him. I could hear the crying from some distance away. A high-pitched squeak so mournful it would break even the hardest of hearts. To my relief, he was not alone. The two boys, always such loyal friends of his mother, were standing protectively over him. Nudging him with their noses every so often to reassure him they were there. I stayed only for a short while; my broken heart couldn't take the crying any longer. But I checked on them every day for the next few weeks until the little orphan eventually stopped sobbing and I was satisfied that he was being protected by his surrogate uncles.

Losing rhinos to poachers is one of the hardest things I have ever had to endure. Sadly, this wasn't the first time I did, and I am sure it won't be the last. Death happens on a daily basis in the bush, it is the natural cycle of life. But the unnecessary, and often, brutal death of these peaceful, compassionate creatures is simply intolerable. So, I am always zealous about trying any methods possible to put an end to it.

One year, we had the opportunity to trial some state-of-the-art horn implants that would communicate directly with my cell phone. The implants would alert me to any suspicious activity going on with the implanted rhino that might indicate the presence of poachers. While they weren't designed to prevent a rhino coming to harm, they might allow us to catch the poachers in the act.

A hole had to be drilled into the horn of the sedated rhino. The implant, not much bigger than a packet of chewing gum, was then inserted. The hole was sealed with dental acrylic that had been dyed the same colour as the horn. Once sealed, the implant was virtually undetectable. We had two implants to test and decided to target two females, as males are more prone to fighting which might damage the implant, or set off too many false alarms.

The first job was to find and dart the rhino from a helicopter. While the ground team and I waited in vehicles ready to respond, the vet and the pilot set off in search of suitable females. We didn't want one that was with a calf as that would leave it vulnerable during the operation and for a short time afterwards while she was still recovering from the tranquiliser.

It wasn't long before we received word from the helicopter that they had darted the first rhino. When the location was verified, we sped off to reach the animal before the drugs took effect. Unfortunately, when we arrived, we found it was not a female, but a young male. Identifying rhino from the air, while the helicopter is spinning at break-neck speed and the rhino is dodging under bushes, is incredibly hard. It was an entirely understandable mistake, especially for people not familiar with the individual rhinos on the reserve. The young male was not a suitable candidate for the implant, but we took the opportunity to microchip the animal anyway in the event that he was poached and the horn recovered, it could be traced back to this individual.

While the ground team waited for the rhino to recover from the sedation, the Reserve Manager asked that I help the pilot locate a female. I knew the rhinos on the reserve better than anyone, and would have been able to pick out suitable candidates more easily. Flying in a helicopter is my greatest guilty pleasure - guilty because of the gross environmental impact of it. Flying in an open-sided game capture helicopter is like that pleasure on steroids. The speed and angles at which these nippy helicopters can fly, under the ludicrous skill of the pilots, is beyond measure. I find the freedom of that movement breath-taking. While not remotely peaceful - helicopters are absurdly loud - I think it is the closest a human can get to the agility and control of a bird in the air.

After a few minutes of enjoying looping around, I set to work finding a rhino. After turning down a couple of options, based on their sex or presence of young calves, I eventually spotted a female I knew fitted the bill perfectly. Once darted, the pilot skilfully herded the girl into the road where she eventually dropped in the ideal position for the ground team to get to work. Once they were on scene, we set off in search of a second candidate. Again, passing over a couple of youngsters, we eventually found another suitable female, so we looped back to fetch the vet.

On our way back, we spotted the male we had darted earlier, looking distinctly unconscious under a tree. Worried that he was in difficulty, as opposed to just asleep, I tried to radio the ground team but couldn't reach anyone.

"Can you drop me on the ground so I can go alert the vet that this rhino might be in trouble?" I asked the pilot.

Not wanting to cover the ground team in dust, the pilot lowered us to the ground about 500 metres down the road. Before the helicopter had even touched the ground, I leapt out and was running, head ducked, away from the still spinning rotors. I could see the ground team on the brow of a hill in the road and set off towards them. I noticed a couple of them waving. I tried to shout that the male rhino was down, but my voice was drowned out by the rotor noise of the helicopter that was still coming to a stop.

The waving seemed to be getting more frantic and now I could see, but not hear, the team was also shouting back at me. I started to wonder what was going on, I was the one coming with urgent news. *What on earth are they trying to tell me that is so important*? Then, I realised it wasn't so much waving as exaggerated pointing, towards something on my right.

While still running up the hill, I looked to my right just in time to see the female rhino they had been working on, charging straight towards me. It seemed they had finished the operation and the rhino was very much awake. She appeared to be pissed off at the intrusion and wanted to take it out on whatever sucker gave her the opportunity. Unfortunately for me, I had ended up in the wrong place at the wrong time and had been singled out as that sucker.

With the momentum from running still propelling me, I veered off to the left into the bushes. In a split second, I scanned the trees, managing to spot a non-thorny bushwillow that was potentially scalable. Without even thinking, I started to climb and was a couple of metres off the ground when the rhino came crashing through the undergrowth beneath me.

I hung on for a few more minutes until I was sure she was gone, thinking to myself, *Hey I just climbed a tree!* I guess, all it takes is being chased up one by an angry rhino.

A truck pulled up next to me.

"Need a ride?" the driver asked, mockingly.

"Yes, please," I replied casually, as I descended from my perch. "Now get your arses down to where we darted that male earlier. He's passed out again under the tree."

> *"And one day she discovered that
> she was fierce, and strong, and full of fire,
> and that not even she could hold herself back
> because her passion burned brighter
> than her fears."*
>
> - Marc Anthony[11]

Chapter 10

It's Not the Wildlife You Need to Worry About

```
TEXT RECEIVED [25:07:2015, 08:58:04]
ROSIE:  Hi Mum. Can I come home for a bit…
```

As crazy as some of these encounters sound, now that I know what I am doing, it's not the wildlife I am worried about. I know how to behave in order to minimise the risks and do so accordingly. For the most part, animals are not out to get us. They generally prefer to avoid people altogether. Of course, freak accidents can and do happen, but ask anyone who lives and works in the bush and they will likely say they feel safer walking alone in the wild than driving down a busy motorway. Statistically speaking, they are.

But when you add people to the mix it's a different story. Humans are unpredictable, and unpredictability in the bush is dangerous.

When rhino poaching was at its peak, I felt an overwhelming sense of hopelessness and a lack of control. And I hated it. I needed to do something, anything, to feel like I was making a difference. So, when there was a tip-off that poachers were coming one evening, I volunteered to spend all night out with the anti-poaching team on a sting operation - armed with nothing but a can of pepper spray.

I undertook night-time anti-poaching patrols every week, but normally, my role was to drive around overtly, shining a spotlight to make a big show that people were active on the reserve. The purpose was to act as a deterrent, as opposed to trying to actually catch poachers. This time, however, I was going incognito with the very real possibility of coming face-to-face with poachers.

I was stationed close to the road where we had been told the poachers would be entering. With my vehicle hidden in some bushes, a colleague and I sat in complete silence waiting in the dark. When you wait for something to happen for hours in the darkness, the silence becomes deafening and every muscle in your body becomes twitchy. I could hear my blood pulsing rhythmically through my veins. *Thud, thud, thud.* The tiniest movement of my arm or leg seemed to make an excruciatingly loud sound. But the stiller and quieter I tried to be, the twitchier and louder I felt I was.

The agony of being silent was soon broken, though, when shortly after the time we had been given by the informant, a crack split the night air in two. If you have ever heard a high-powered rifle fire at close range, you will understand it is not just a loud noise. You can actually sense the shockwaves passing through the air. They penetrate your body and rattle every single one of your cells. The entire environment around you reacts too. Like when a bomb goes off or an earthquake strikes, the wildlife responds a split second before you register what is happening. Birds take off, and insects fall quiet. And after the shockwave passes, there is a moment of eerie stillness. Then, the world comes rushing back to your consciousness again. Your ears go into overdrive and the sounds of the night flood your senses in a torrent.

"Shit! Was that a rifle shot?" I whispered, breaking the muteness we had held for the past couple of hours. "That can't have been much more than a hundred metres away?"

My colleague grabbed the radio and called the head of anti-poaching.

"Gunshot fired. Did you hear?" he asked.

"Yes, copy. We are on our way. Stay put and listen for any movement."

A million thoughts raced through my head. *Why did they fire just there, there aren't any rhino around here at the moment? What if they are coming our way and walk right into us? What should we do?* I felt my grip tighten around the can of pepper spray and squinted into the darkness, willing my night vision to be better.

Over the next hour, the radio murmured away as the anti-poaching team reported in from their various locations. We sensed no further activity in our vicinity and the anti-poaching team reported there was no sign of poachers having entered the reserve. From our position, the crack had appeared to have come from just outside the fence. The head of anti-poaching explained to us that sometimes poachers will fire a distraction shot in one location, attracting a response from the anti-poaching team, to allow another group of poachers to enter on the other side of the reserve undetected. But, the team had remained spread out around the reserve to prevent that from happening. It is also possible that the poachers themselves had been tipped off that we had been informed - a double bluff, so to speak -

and fired a shot to see whether there was a team on standby waiting to ambush. Maybe, it hadn't been poachers at all.

Whatever the situation, it seemed that the rhino would be safe for another night at least. At 4 a.m., we were dismissed from our post and drove back home in silence. I think we were both reconsidering our decision to assist the anti-poaching team that night. The thought of coming face-to-face with armed poachers was a little too far out of my comfort zone. I'd rather take a charging rhino any day of the week.

It's not just the people that may intentionally want to cause you harm that are the problem though. Being around inexperienced people in the bush makes things unpredictable and difficult to manage the risks.

Part of training as a guide is learning how to manage people. Most guides will tell you, interpreting animal behaviour is the easy bit. When on your own in the bush, it is relatively simple to keep yourself alive. But throw in the unpredictability of other people and the situation changes. Half the marks in the practical assessments at guiding school centre around how you manage guests in various high-stress situations.

During my practical assessment drive, I briefly left the vehicle to follow some leopard tracks. On my return, I found half my guests missing and the rest pretending to eat poisonous berries. This had just been a prank to test my nerves, and I was able to round up my guests again to the satisfaction of the assessor, but I learnt a valuable lesson that day – do not assume everyone has the same level of common sense.

The final test in the Advanced Rifle Handling assessment which is one of the qualifications you need to take guests into the bush on foot, is called the simulated charge. It involves you taking a group of proxy guests on a walk in the bush, armed with a .375 rifle loaded with live rounds. As you are walking along, pointing out different birds and trees to your guests, an animal bursts out of the bushes and charges you - in this instance, it is a cardboard cut-out on a pulley system.

Without taking your eyes off the animal, you must shout at your guests, "Stay behind me! Stand still!" While you are shouting at your guests, the noise has another important function of intimidating the approaching animal. At the same time, you must stand tall and face the animal, kick up sand and throw rocks. Anything you can, to try make the animal think twice about taking you on. In the majority of cases, this works and the animal will pull up or veer off. But in the assessment, it doesn't. It keeps charging.

At 20-metres distance, you must cock your rifle. The metal clank of a cartridge inserting into the chamber of a bolt-action rifle is often enough noise to stop an animal and make it turn around. But, this time, it keeps charging.

Without looking behind you, you must know exactly where all your guests are and whether any of them are on the verge of running. You must shout again to your guests, "Stay behind me!" as you take aim and prepare to fire.

The cardboard cut-out is a lion, so you know that when shooting it from a standing position you risk firing over the top of its head, which is bobbing up and down with its running motion. So you must get down on one knee giving yourself a better angle.

The lion is ten metres away and showing no signs of stopping. You now have less than one second to take your shot, and it needs to be a direct hit to the brain to stop the animal in its tracks. Otherwise, momentum will provide you with an injured lion in your lap. You squeeze the trigger, *CRACK*, the recoil punches you in the shoulder, but there's no time to acknowledge that, you need to fire off a second, insurance round. The hours of training have ingrained the action into muscle memory. Without even thinking, you lift the bolt lever, yank it back, ejecting the spent cartridge, then push the bolt lever forwards and down again, chambering the next round. There's no time to think about taking aim, it needs to be done instinctively. You squeeze the trigger again. *CRACK*.

The lion stops dead.

Still not taking your eyes off the animal, you ask your guests if they are ok, warning them again to keep back and stand still. You cautiously approach the lion, ejecting your second spent cartridge and chambering a third round as you go. You poke the animal with the rifle. It doesn't move. You poke it in the eye, there is no reflex reaction. It is dead. Before turning to face your guests, you eject the round from the chamber and make your rifle safe. The assessment is over.

The whole thing happens in a blink of an eye and the actions you take are carried out almost without thinking - the protocols have been rehearsed so many times it has become automated behaviour.

But, under the pressure of the realistic simulation, mistakes can happen. If at any point you shout, "Don't run!" at your guests, you fail. Human brains are funny things, so often people will only hear the word "run" and before you know it, your guests are legging it, making themselves the more enticing target for the charging animal.

If you turn to face your guests while the rifle is loaded, you fail. But if any of your guests move and you don't notice and bring them back under control, you also fail.

If you don't try to intimidate the animal before firing, giving it a chance to change its mind, you fail.

If you don't fire a second, insurance shot before the animal smacks you in the face, you fail.

There are a multitude of other reasons you can fail the assessment. But, most obviously, if you did not in fact hit your target, you fail.

I made my rifle safe and turned to face the assessors. They signalled that the assessment was completed and everyone could stand down. Then, they came to join me at my fallen victim to check my shot placement. I had been consistently accurate all throughout my training and in the previous rounds of the assessment. True to form, my two holes were overlapping each other. Perfect grouping. Unfortunately, they were not in the brain. They were centimetres left of the mark, in the shoulder.

I had failed.

Months of practice had gotten me that far. I spent hours each afternoon practicing loading and unloading the rifle and aiming at targets to instil the action into my muscle memory. But when I realised I had failed the final test, I wasn't disappointed. I felt relieved. I was happy to only be qualified to guide from a vehicle. I didn't want people's lives in my hands in such an unpredictable environment as on foot. Not because of the unpredictability of the animals though, because of the unpredictability of people you are responsible for.

I am sure, sitting comfortably at home, you are thinking, *I would never do anything as stupid as walk towards some lions*. But, intelligent and normally sensible people do. I once had a group run straight towards the sound of lions roaring in the darkness. The only way I could turn them around was to ring the dinner bell - the group was entirely made up of strapping, young lads and thankfully the draw of food trumped the excitement of seeing lions.

I guess you might say the guides are partially to blame. We do such a good job at making everything seem safe that people under our care become complacent. While I do know some phenomenal guides, who are far braver and more skilful than me, none of them are superhuman. There are limits to our powers to keep people safe.

But of course, as I moved up the ranks and ended up managing projects, it didn't matter that I wasn't the one physically taking the guests or volunteers out on foot, I was still ultimately responsible. I was responsible 24/7 no matter what the situation. I was responsible when one of my team came back from a drive, ashen-faced and told me a volunteer had exited the car at a lion sighting. I was responsible when a volunteer walked around outside in the dark, talking on the phone, not paying the slightest bit of attention to the world around them - ignoring the fact that there had been both a hippo and a leopard in the garden the previous night. I was responsible when a volunteer was bitten by a snake in the night but didn't tell anyone until the next morning.

I was responsible even if I wasn't actually there at the time. I was responsible even if I was asleep. I was responsible even though safety briefings were given and risk assessments had been covered in painstaking detail, explaining the do's and don'ts of living in the bush. And after a while, this level of responsibility started to take its toll.

I was in my third year of managing the volunteer project, and the job was feeling less and less like guiding and educating, and more like babysitting. Rarely a day passed when I wasn't dealing with someone's issues. If it wasn't someone injured playing volleyball, it was someone with an upset stomach. If it wasn't someone unhappy with the meal choice that day, it was someone wanting to switch groups to be with their BFF. Being in my mid-thirties, with the majority of the volunteers under 25, I was losing touch with them. In the beginning, we had no electricity and everyone sat around chatting and playing cards in the soft glow of lanterns. But by this point, we had power and even the internet. The first thing volunteers would ask was "What's the WiFi password? I want to Snapchat my friends." I didn't even know what Snapchat was. It was sapping the enjoyment out of life in the bush. My work permit was due to expire later that year, and so I started to question whether I wanted to apply for a renewal, or if it was time to move on.

As soon as I started thinking about leaving, there was a flurry of incidents that helped me make that decision. As if the gods were giving me signs to say "Yes, it is time for you to go now."

It started with a call on the radio from the neighbouring camp, requesting first aid assistance. Being the qualified first aid instructor in camp, I volunteered to go. I grabbed my first aid kit and headed off. On the way, I wondered what injury I might be dealing with. I was imagining a serious wound that would need pressure bandaging. I was trying to remember whether I had enough bandages in the small kit I had on the seat next to me. However, when I arrived, it was clear my bandaging skills were not required. The situation was much more dire.

'Help! Over here. She's not breathing." A man was waving me over.

I sprinted from my car and, without even asking any questions, started giving CPR. Just like with the rifle, I had practiced CPR so many times, teaching it to the new volunteers every single month for the past few years, that it was automated. No thinking was required.

Only once I was in the swing of it did I start to ask questions. The patient was the man's wife. He was the only other person here. The lady that had radioed me for help, had left to get phone signal to call for an ambulance. He didn't know what had happened. They just heard a yelp and found her at the bottom of the steps like this.

"Please help her. I don't know what to do. I can feel she's still warm. You have to save her." He kept pleading with me to help.

There were no signs of life, and I wasn't sure anything I was doing was helping. But, that was irrelevant. I did what I had to do, if not for her, then for her husband. I carried on giving CPR until the paramedics arrived an hour-and-a-half later when they pronounced her dead. I felt numb and awkward.

They asked that I stay until the coroner and police arrived as they would want to take my statement. I just wanted to leave the situation and have a cold shower to wash the whole tragedy off me. While the adrenaline of the event had given me the strength to keep going with the CPR for so long, now I had stopped, the exhaustion hit me like a tidal wave. I sat back against a rock and only then realised my knees were bleeding and there was gravel embedded deep into the skin. I got up and walked to the kitchen tap, and washed my face, hands and knees. And then sat at the edge of camp until I was needed for the interviews. I didn't want to look the man in the face, I didn't want to see his pain. By the time the police had finished with me, it was dark. When I got home, I went straight for a shower and then lay on my bed in the darkness. I didn't feel like talking to anyone about what had happened.

A short while later, I had a rare day off. I was in town doing some shopping, when I got a call from camp.

"Rosie, there's been an accident. They have rolled the minibus. You are closest, can you go see what the situation is?"

I put my shopping basket down and rushed out of the shop without paying. The road back out of town was long and straight, so I could see the minibus from a fair distance away. It was on the side of the road, facing the wrong way and turned over on its side. As I got closer, I could see it had flattened a couple of the wooden stalls that sold fruit and vegetables on the roadside. *Oh God!* I thought. It looked like carnage, and I was fearing the worst.

I found the driver behind the minibus, sitting on his haunches with his head in his hands. Apart from a few cuts and scrapes he, miraculously, seemed ok.

"Are you ok? Is anyone else injured?" I had hold of his shoulders, trying to give him a once over.

"I'm ok. No one else is hurt," he said. "I don't know what happened. One minute I was passing that truck, and the next I was upside down." He was clearly shaken.

Some witnesses came forward and said that the truck had clipped the rear end of the minibus, sending it into a tailspin. On hitting the verge, the bus tipped over and slid into the stalls on its side. Fortunately, the vendors had not been in the stalls at the time, but they were understandably upset at the damage.

By the time the police released us from the scene and the bus had been towed away, it was too late to go back to town and finish my shopping. *So much for my day off,* I thought. But it could have been a lot worse, as I was soon to find out.

Once a month, we would make the 12-hour round trip to Johannesburg to drop off departing volunteers and pick up new ones. Normally, two of us would go so as to share the driving duties. Now without our own minibus, I had to hire a transfer company to do the trip for us, and I went alone as a passenger.

On top of the two serious accidents, in the previous couple of months there had been disciplinary hearings, punch-ups between staff and an ever-increasing number of poaching incidents. I had been having sleepless nights and feeling like things were spiralling out of control. I had a niggling feeling of impending doom, so it was a relief to not be the one driving to Johannesburg. It is treacherous journey involving potholes large enough to swallow a car, cows randomly lying in the road and highly reckless drivers.

On the way up to the city, the vehicle was silent and everyone, except the driver, slept. I took the opportunity to re-energise before having to put on the welcoming, smiley face for the new arrivals we were collecting.

The return journey was a lot livelier, with the new volunteers excited about embarking on the experience of a lifetime. It was a big group, so the bus was full. We had even brought a trailer for the luggage. I sat in the front passenger seat facing backwards in order to engage with the volunteers and answer their myriad of questions. After a few hours, even they were flagging, many having travelled for hours, if not days to reach South Africa. So eventually, I swivelled back in my seat and dozed off again.

"No, no, no!"

I woke up with a start. The driver was yelling.

In the road ahead of us, coming around a bend, was a large haulage truck, with a smaller car on its flanks. The car was overtaking on the bend and was in our lane. The car swerved to our left, straddling our lane and the verge of the road. But this still did not leave us enough room on the road. Our driver tried to steer the minibus between the oncoming car and the truck, but the momentum of the bus and the trailer combined carried us over into the other lane. We were on course for a head-on collision with the truck.

I don't know how long it took before the impact came, it can only have been a fraction of a second. But it felt like minutes, and I felt oddly serene. I was resigned to the fact that there was absolutely nothing I could do about my situation. I knew I was about to die and I didn't try to fight it. I wasn't scared. It was curiously calming. I was angry, but only because I definitely did not want to die in a boring car crash. *How unjust, given the death-defying life I lead.*

I instinctively put my hands up in front of my face, bracing for the impact. The world went dark and quiet.

The next thing I remember was feeling weightless, like I was flying. *So, this is what it is like to be dead.* But before I could appreciate the sensation, I felt a jolt. The crunching of metal, the shattering of glass and the screaming of voices brought me back down to earth. *Oh, not dead then.* My body was being thrown around like I was in a bumper car. I opened my eyes, but I still couldn't see anything. I realised my head was enveloped in the airbag and I punched it away from my face. Once free from its suffocating rubber, I gulped in deep breaths. *I feel nothing, no pain at all. Can I really be ok?*

I looked to my right, I could barely see the driver. He had taken the brunt of the impact and was now buried under the metal and plastic of the dashboard. He was locking eyes with me and asking, "Is everyone ok?" Utter terror was etched across his face.

I tried to turn around to see, but I realised I was also pinned under the dashboard that was now resting on my thighs. I twisted my neck as far as it would go and shouted, "Is everyone ok? Is everyone ok?"

People were already up and out of their seats trying to get out of the bus. But the impact had buckled the sides and the sliding doors wouldn't open.

"Rosie, get us out. We need to get out," someone was calling, panic-stricken. I tried my door, but it was also jammed closed. The window wouldn't budge either.

"I'm trapped," I called back. "You need to smash the back window and climb out."

By now, some other cars had arrived at the scene. I called out to them asking them to direct traffic as, I realised, we were sitting sideways across both lanes on a blind corner. One man helped break the back window and lifted the volunteers out.

Still unable to move my legs, I rummaged around blindly at my feet for my phone. It had been on my lap at the time of impact, so I figured it must have flown forwards into the footwell. I eventually found it but the screen was blank other than an exclamation mark indicating there had been an error. *So much for the military grade, drop-proof case!* Just as I was berating it, and wondering how I was going to raise the alarm, the phone came back to life. *Thank God!*

A car accident on the airport run was a scenario we rehearsed for regularly. Our boss had repeatedly said it would be his worst nightmare and wanted to make sure we were prepared for any eventuality. Following the emergency protocols, I dialled his number first, initiating the communication tree that would get the emergency services to us.

"Hi," I said. "Your worst nightmare has just happened."

I gave him the details of our location and the situation as far as I could tell at that point in time.

He would call us back once the emergency services were on their way. Then, I levered my seat back as far as it would go and finally managed to free my legs out from under the dashboard. Crawling over the back of my chair, I could finally see the situation in the back of the bus. Broken glass and people's belongings were strewn everywhere. But I was relieved to see that all the seats were empty and everyone had managed to climb out the back of the bus.

A stranger approached me, they had just arrived on the scene and explained that they were a doctor, visiting from France. They asked if there was anything they could do. I directed them to the driver, explaining that I didn't know him, but he seemed to be in a pretty bad way. My responsibility was to the volunteers and I had to check them over first before I could do anything else.

The next couple of hours were a blur. I was in constant motion moving from volunteer to volunteer and answering the phone, planning the logistics for getting us out of the predicament we were now in. A crowd grew and people kept asking me questions, but my head was fuzzy and I didn't know if they were the authorities or just the scavenging tow trucks that always seem to arrive at accidents first to fight for the go ahead to remove your vehicle, later sending you a large bill in the mail.

The paramedics arrived and, satisfied that no one in my group was in urgent need of care, focused on stabilising the driver, so the fire brigade could cut him out. A new bus was being sent to collect us, so I instructed everyone to get their luggage out of the trailer and sit on it in a huddle until the rescue bus arrived. It was already getting dark.

You've been in a crash because an idiot overtook on a blind corner and now you will likely get robbed. Welcome to South Africa!

As the time wore on, the chemicals my body had produced to block my pain receptors wore off. What started as a dull ache in my pelvis, became an increasingly acute pain. I walked behind the ambulance, out of sight of the volunteers, and doubled over in agony. One of the paramedics saw me and came over.

"You need to go to the hospital, sister," he said. "They nearly have the driver out, once he is on his way, I am taking you in the second ambulance."

"I can't go, I am responsible for all these people. They only arrived in South Africa a few hours ago, and I am the only person in the country they know." My stubbornness was kicking in. But he wasn't going to negotiate. I did, however, convince him to take the three most injured people in the group with me. I didn't need a whole ambulance to myself.

Once I was sure the recovery bus was less than half an hour away, I gathered the three volunteers coming in the ambulance with me and gave strict instructions to the others to stay put until the bus arrived. It would be bringing them all to the hospital as well, I insisted everyone had to be examined by a doctor.

The hospital was two hours' drive away and it was 4 a.m. by the time everyone had been checked out and cleared. The doctor that examined me lacked the same dry sense of humour I have, so, when he asked how I felt and I replied, "Like I have been hit by a truck," without any reaction, he simply wrote me a prescription for ibuprofen and said I was free to go. I was still more concerned about everyone else and concentrated on making sure they had the required x-rays and examinations.

Once everyone had filled up on canteen sandwiches and juice boxes, the recovery bus transferred us to a nearby hotel and we had a couple of hours' sleep before getting back on the road to head for camp. The replacement driver seemed acutely aware of our nervousness and drove at a snail's pace to camp, the journey taking an agonising four hours. At the time of the crash, we had been only an hour from camp, it seemed cruel that we had backtracked so far only to redo the journey.

Back at camp, the whole team stood in the driveway to welcome us home. I got warm but painful hugs from everyone, relieved that we had made it back in one piece. Normally, I would spend the whole day with the new arrivals, inducting them to camp. But I appealed to my team to excuse me this time, asking them to cover my duties. I called my boss and asked for the rest of the day off. It now seems ludicrous that I even felt I had to ask. I walked wearily to my room. I looked in the mirror and saw I had a huge gash across my neck from the seatbelt. My hair was full of tiny pieces of glass and I had droplets of blood splattered all over me - it wasn't my own blood, it was the driver's, and the thought of this made me recoil. Every inch of my body hurt, and I found it almost impossible to lift my arms above my head to remove my t-shirt. I stepped gingerly into the shower and stood under the steaming water for nearly half-an-hour - letting it wash away the tears from my eyes before they had a chance to form.

After towelling myself down and putting on some clean clothes, I lay down on my bed and fell fast asleep. A couple of hours later, I woke up and decided to text my mum.

"Can I come home for a bit?"

I need a break now. I am tired of all the drama.

> *"A warrior still needs love and affection,*
> *the same way a tiger in the wild does.*
> *Just because we carry strength,*
> *doesn't mean we are always strong."*
> *- Nikki Rowe*[12]

Chapter 11

Going Home

```
TEXT RECEIVED [24:05:2019, 11:22:35]
ROSIE: Hi Mum. The doctor says going back to
the bush is off the cards…
```

I was actually excited to go home. I hadn't lived in the UK for 12 years, and I was nostalgic for the country I had grown up in. After six years of living at my place of work, unable to make a cup of tea without being asked a question, I was also really looking forward to having my own space.

I got a "proper" job, with a large conservation NGO, and went to an office five days a week. I rented a traditional English cottage, and filled it with my non-traditional African artwork and curios, just like my childhood home had been. Where most people have photos of family and friends on their walls, I had photos of my cheetah family. I discovered Netflix, I joined sports clubs, and I went to dinner with friends. I was living a normal, drama-free life again, and at first, it was great. Without the weight of responsibility on my shoulders, I could relax and concentrate on myself for the first time in years.

The world outside my bush bubble was mind-blowing. Having access to everything you could possibly imagine with just one click of a mouse, often on next-day delivery, was inconceivable. It had taken six months to get a new freezer delivered to camp the previous year. I became a shopaholic.

I went to talks and events, festivals and gigs, and watched live sports at every opportunity - all the things that were virtually impossible when living in the bush. I also ate different foods every day - in the bush, we had a pretty limited menu that was only supplemented by the occasional trips into town to eat a steak, burger or pizza. Being able to go to an Ethiopian restaurant one week and eat Greek meze the next, was living the foodie dream.

The kid-in-a-candy-store excitement soon wore off though and, in reality, I struggled to fit in.

In the beginning, it was small, and often amusing, things that caught me out. I found it difficult to drive at an appropriate speed for British roads. I was so used to driving at 20 kmph, scanning the hedgerows on either side of the road for hiding creatures, or investigating every item of roadkill to check if it was something interesting. I would find myself slowing down for oak trees, searching the large boughs for a slumbering leopard. In winter, when horses in the fields were wearing their grey blankets to protect them from the cold, I frequently slammed on my brakes thinking they were rhino. On foot, I was no better. Every rustle in the leaf litter instinctively made me think, *Snake*! I would bemuse my lunchtime walk companions by freezing and staring into the undergrowth every five minutes, only to be disappointed that it was another blackbird or thrush.

There were also less trivial issues.

For a start, I wasn't sure what my identity was. In the bush, I was surrounded by people just like me, no explanations were ever necessary. People rarely asked where I was from, because it was not important. We were all from different places, but we were kindred spirits because we chose to be in the wild.

In the UK, it was different. People were always asking where I was from, puzzled by my mixed-up accent and dialect. I didn't know what the right answer was. No matter what response I gave, it was never satisfactory to the enquirer. "You don't sound like you're from Yorkshire?" I would hear daily. Even though I was living less than ten kilometres from where I had grown up, I felt like an outsider. I didn't belong there, at least, not anymore. Eventually, I came up with the answer that I was nomadic. It was easier to say that than explain the convoluted route I had taken through life that meant I sounded vaguely and generically English, but with an Antipodean twang and used a dialogue peppered with South African idioms like *"Is it,"* *"Ag shame,"* *"Eish,"* and *"Just now."* The dominant component of my accent changing depending on who I had been talking to most recently.

It wasn't that the enquiries were ever negative or accusatory. If anything, my unconventional life story intrigued people. I was a curiosity and people wanted to hear my tales. But, engaging with people in stories about the bush can be exhausting. Unless you have lived that life, you can't really understand what it is like. People who haven't experienced it for themselves tend to see the danger and the magic in all the wrong things.

Beyond telling my stories, integration with my new cohort was difficult because I couldn't contribute to everyday conversations. I didn't know anything about popular culture and world politics. I hadn't watched TV or seen a new movie in years. I had been living an insular life, where the only world-scale problem I knew about was rhino poaching. It upset me that no one seemed to know that there was even a poaching crisis going on in South Africa.

I was frustrated when people moaned about frivolous things like the wrong hummus in the cafeteria or Southern Rail cancelling trains. The dangers of living in the bush, and South Africa in general, are often exaggerated. But still, I had never had so little to worry about that the ingredients of a dip had become an important topic of conversation.

The problem was that with each passing month, I was becoming that person, too. I moaned all the time that the trains were late. I drove the extra couple of kilometres to shops that had the specific brands I liked. I was losing perspective about what was important to me and I was losing my hardened, wild edge. I didn't like it. I didn't want to be like everyone else. I didn't want to be ordinary. There came a point when I realised I didn't actually want to integrate because I didn't want to belong in that world.

After two years of relying on people I had met in South Africa for solace, meeting up whenever possible or simply spending endless hours reminiscing on WhatsApp, I finally got the chance to travel to Kenya for work. It had been 18 years since I had last touched down in Nairobi, but it felt anything but unfamiliar. Stepping off the plane, I had the same feeling I get every time I land on the continent - I was home. Here, I was not an outsider. Here, I was in my element.

The few weeks I had in Kenya flew by, but I had a smile on my face for every second of it. From the red elephants of Tsavo to the views of Mount Kenya, it all felt so familiar and I felt my heart was at peace once more. Waiting for my flight back to the UK was agony. *I don't want to go back. I want to stay here.* I had to find a way to get back to the bush.

Over the course of the following year, I kept plugging away, making contacts everywhere I could, putting out feelers for opportunities. My stubbornness eventually paid off. Just over a year after I came back from Kenya, I landed a job managing a carnivore project in Botswana.

I was finally going back to where I belong, back to the bush.

A few weeks later, I went on my routine lunchtime walk with a colleague, no longer jumping at blackbirds in the undergrowth. We were walking up a very slight slope when I started to get out of breath. *Weird*! I thought, given how fit I was at the time. I pushed on, but soon I was seeing stars, then nothing but blackness. Next, my hearing went as if I had put my head under water.

"I think I am going to pass out." I wasn't sure if I had even said it out loud at first because the sound appeared to be only in my head, but then I felt a steadying hand of my friend on my elbow. I crouched down on my haunches and stuck my head between my knees. Very quickly my senses returned to normal.

"Are you ok?"

"Yeah, I just felt very faint. I'm fine now. Let's carry on."

We continued on our walk, but I had a niggling thought in the back of my mind that, despite taking deep gulping breaths, I wasn't getting the required amount of oxygen to my brain. On returning to the office, halfway up the stairs to my cubicle, I felt the stars coming back.

"Maybe it's the pollen in the air?" I said half trying to convince myself. "It's making me a bit wheezy." But I knew it wasn't. I wasn't struggling to breathe, I was suffocating.

Back at my desk, I tried to distract myself by getting stuck into what I had been working on before lunch. Within half-an-hour, I had a cracking headache and my skin felt clammy. I knew I wasn't well.

"Actually, I think I am just going to work from home this afternoon," I informed my team, packing up my things. "I need to lie down for a bit."

It was only a five-minute drive back to my cottage, and I was grateful I had driven that morning and not cycled like I normally did. But when I reached my driveway, something inside me told me to keep on driving. *I need to see a doctor.*

I walked into the reception at the doctor's surgery and stumbled forwards into the counter. Feeling like I was going to pass out again, I whispered, "I don't feel well. I need to see someone please."

The receptionist was halfway through explaining that there was a long queue and the doctor may not be able to see me today, when a nurse jumped in and said, "I'll take a look at her, she really doesn't look well."

She took me to her room and told me to lie down on the bed. While I described my symptoms, she quickly started taking my vital signs and hooked me up to an ECG to measure my heart activity.

"Hmmm, how are you feeling now?" she asked.

"Better," I replied, honestly. I felt normal again pretty soon after lying down.

"Your blood pressure, heart rate, oxygen saturation and ECG are all within normal range. But you really didn't look right to me when you came in. Are you generally quite fit and active?"

"Yes, I run or go to the gym every day," I explained. "I'm training to do a 10k." I looked at the blood pressure monitor and added, "Normally, my blood pressure is really low, that's actually quite high for me."

"Ok, let me go talk to the doctor briefly." She left the room, and I lay back, anxious about what could be wrong with me.

The nurse had been gone for an uncomfortably long time. I jumped when she eventually re-entered the room. "The doctor thinks you are probably fine, but I bullied him into sending you for a quick blood test because I said I wasn't happy. But you'll have to go to the hospital to do it. Is that ok?"

"Sure." I gathered up my things, and after the nurse handed me the paperwork for the blood test, headed to my car. At the hospital, I didn't have to wait long for the blood to be drawn, but assuming the results would take hours, if not days, to come back, I set off for home again.

I was just pulling in my driveway when my phone rang. It was the doctor.

"Rosemary Miles?"

"Yes."

"Where are you?"

"At home."

"Ok, listen to me carefully. You need to go back to hospital immediately. Go straight to the Emergency Department. They are expecting you. And, don't drive."

"Ok. What's going on?"

"The blood tests indicate that you have a significant blood clot somewhere in your body, and given you were struggling to breathe earlier, it is most likely in your lungs. It is urgent. Do you understand?"

"Um... yes. Ok. I will go now."

A friend dropped me at the entrance to the hospital where I was met by a nurse with a needle in her hand.

"Rosemary, we were expecting you. I am just going to inject you with this heparin. It will help prevent any more clotting while we run other tests and work out what's actually going on. Lift your shirt, please."

There was a sharp prick in my belly, followed by a stinging sensation.

"Don't rub or scratch it," she added. "It will make the stinging worse."

She hooked me up to all the same paraphernalia as the previous nurse and commented that my heart rate and blood pressure were slightly elevated but within normal range. I explained, again, that normally they are both much lower.

A short while later they called me in to see the doctor.

"This is quite puzzling. Other than shortness of breath, you are not displaying any other signs of clots. But your D-dimer test, which indicates the presence of clotting in your blood, was more than ten times the reference level." He went on, "You aren't a typical candidate for a pulmonary embolism - that's a blood clot in your lungs - you are young, fit, a non-smoker. Are you taking the contraceptive pill?"

"Yes, for like the past 20 years," I shrugged.

"Ah, well that's probably it. I assume you were informed of the risk of blood clotting from the contraceptive pill?" I shrugged. I couldn't really recall that information ever being impressed upon me. I was always told I had such low blood pressure that I was not a high risk for complications associated with the pill.

The doctor continued, "Anyway, I am going to send you for more blood tests, a chest x-ray, and an ultrasound of your leg - as the clot can often start in your leg. I see in your notes you were complaining of leg pain a few weeks ago. After that, we'll do a CT scan of your lungs. Once we have those results back, we'll know what we are dealing with."

Over the next 12 hours, I was poked, prodded and pricked repeatedly. I had radioactive contrast injected into my veins and was passed through the CT scanner. Every couple of hours, my oxygen levels were checked and I was asked how I was feeling. "Fine." I would reply, but on the inside my anxiety levels were skyrocketing. Finally, I was called back in to see the doctor.

"Ok Rosie, so the CT scan shows that your lungs are absolutely riddled with clots. Luckily, they are all small ones and we caught them before they got dangerously large. But, every segment of your lungs contains clots." As he spoke, he was drawing a sketch of my lungs, marking with a dot where all the clots were. It looked like my lungs had measles. "I am honestly quite surprised you are not feeling worse. You seem to be coping remarkably with such significantly reduced lung capacity. I guess because you are so fit."

At this point, I hadn't really taken in the gravity of the situation. Having grown up with an NHS doctor in the house, I have always had faith in medical science. I was waiting for the doctor to give me my medicine and tell me that I'd be better in a week or two.

"We wouldn't bother with surgery to remove clots of this size."

My ears pricked up. *Surgery? This sounds more serious than I thought.*

"Your body will eventually break down the clots itself, or not. Clots this small may never fully disappear, your body might then make its own bypasses around them." He was editing his sketch to show the arteries in my lungs diverting around the dots.

"But we have to make sure no more clots form and these existing ones don't get any bigger. I will be putting you on a course of anticoagulants for the next six months, and then we'll see what the situation is after that."

"Six months!" I blurted.

"Yes, maybe longer," he replied. "You should start feeling better in about a month or so, but once you have had clots, there's a good chance they will come back in the first six months to a year."

"So, what does this mean?" I asked. "I'm supposed to be leaving for Botswana in a month. Can I go?"

"No, absolutely not. You should not fly for the next six months at least."

He carried on listing things I should and shouldn't do, things that will increase or decrease my risk. I had zoned out and didn't hear the rest of the instructions. All I could think about was that I wasn't going back to the wild.

He handed me a prescription and pointed me in the direction of the dispensary. In a daze, I trudged my way down the corridor. *This can't be happening. I have to go back to the bush. I have to.*

While waiting for my medication, I took my phone from my bag and texted my mum. She called me back straight away, but the lump in my throat was so big I couldn't speak. I just hung up. I composed myself and then called her back.

"Why don't you get on the next train and come home. You can go over your medical notes with Dad and get a better understanding of what the situation is. Don't worry, darling. We'll find a way through."

Fortunately, my new employers agreed to put my job on hold for the time-being, allowing me to do some work remotely, while I recovered. Over the next few weeks and months, I read everything I could find on pulmonary emboli and clotting risks. I stubbornly did everything I could to speed up my recovery and reduce the risk of new clots forming. I was back running within a couple of months and was soon as fit, if not fitter, than I had been before the episode. I saw specialists and gave more blood samples than I ever thought possible, all in an attempt to prove that I could recover more quickly than the six months prescribed. It was all in vain. The test results showed that while the contraceptive pill had been the likely trigger, I had an underlying genetic mutation of one of the clotting factors in my blood, making it more likely that I could get clots again in the future. The specialist's advice was to wait until the six months were up to see whether my clotting factors were down to acceptable levels again. Then, we could decide what to do.

It was out of my hands. I had to wait and try not to lose hope.

Six months after my initial diagnosis, I took my last anticoagulant. I celebrated by sending a photo of the last pill in the packet to all my friends and family. I had been taking them religiously every 12 hours since I left the hospital. Taking the last one felt like a milestone. My life, that had been on hold for six months, could finally begin again.

Or, so I thought.

The celebrations were slightly premature. The doctor explained I had to wait four weeks for the medication to work its way out of my system, before going for the final set of blood tests. It was four weeks of anxious anticipation, a three-hour round trip in the snow to give what felt like a pint of my blood, followed by another ten days waiting for the results. Eventually, the results came in and the doctor called with the news - my clotting factors were still slightly elevated.

To say I was disappointed is an understatement. The rollercoaster of emotions that I had been dealing with for the previous few weeks was still in motion. *What does this mean now?*

I was back with the specialist who was reviewing my results. She went through the different scenarios, detailing the risks and benefits of each. I am sure there were some sane options that most other people would have chosen, but the only one I really heard was, "If you go back on the anti-coagulants indefinitely, and take the appropriate precautions to minimise your risks, I don't think it would be unreasonable for you to go to Botswana now. We can review your situation again in 12 months."

That was all I needed to hear. Risk-management is my speciality. If I can learn to live with snakes and elephants on my doorstep, then there's no reason I can't learn to live in the bush with this health condition and just manage the risks accordingly.

True to form, my stubborn spirit kicked in and there was no stopping me. I rushed home and pulled together all the information I needed to satisfy myself, and the medical insurers, that the risks were manageable. Needless to say, the actual risk specialists weren't as convinced as I was, and I spent a week calling every insurance company listed to find someone to cover me. The answers ranged from "We are not willing under any circumstances to insure you" to "We are not worried about your medical condition, but we are not happy that your job involves working with lions." I persisted and eventually found a company that would provide me with the cover I needed. Paperwork sorted, I booked a flight departing in three days' time, determined not to let any other delays have the opportunity to emerge.

My suitcase, that had been sitting empty at the end of my bed for weeks, could finally be packed.
I looked out the window at the snow-covered hills as I packed my khaki shorts and wide-brimmed hat once again. A huge grin spread across my face, I was going home - back to the wild.

> *"Don't tell a girl with fire in her veins*
> *and hurricane bones*
> *what she should and shouldn't do.*
> *In the blink of an eye,*
> *she will shatter that ridiculous cage*
> *you attempt to build around*
> *her beautiful bohemian spirit."*
>
> *- Melody Lee*[13]

Epilogue

*"You have to risk a little crazy
if you ever hope to escape the
gravitational pull of the ordinary."*
- David Usher[14]

So, that's it. I am heading back to my natural habitat. Back to the wild. Twenty years on from when I first set foot on the continent, and ten years since I arrived to train as a guide.

Of course, some people will think I am crazy to move to a country where I know no one and to live in a tent. Especially to be so far away from medical facilities with my underlying health condition. But for me, staying in a conventional office job and living in British suburbia comes with a much greater risk - the risk of watching life pass me by while my wild spirit fades away.

From that first time I set foot in the bush I knew it was where I belonged. It is hard to explain that feeling to someone unless they have experienced it for themselves. It's not that I don't enjoy being in other places, I love lots of things about life in the city too. But it's about where I am most at home, where I feel most like myself.

I envy those that grew up in the bush. I arrived here late in life and via a rather circuitous route. The decision to study astrophysics had been driven by my desire to always be different and unexpected. If I had followed my heart at 18 and studied biology or veterinary science instead, I may have ended up here sooner. And maybe then I would not have to prove myself every day to gain the same respect as those with relevant degrees under their belt. But if I hadn't taken this more challenging road to get here, would I be as strong and determined as I am today? I certainly don't think I would be as good at my job. My meandering course has given me a more rounded, holistic understanding of the world - and of myself.

Of course I have moments of anxiety, wondering if I shouldn't have more money in the bank and a pension plan? *Shouldn't I own my own home by now, instead of living in a tent? What will I have to fall back on when I am too decrepit to wander around the bush anymore?* By the very nature of the conservation industry, a bush life and being nomadic normally go hand-in-hand. People often have the perception that this transient lifestyle is romantic and freeing. In some ways it is, but it can also be exhausting. You never know how long you will get to stay in your new home before you have to move on. Saying goodbye to friends brings constant heartache. And, I have spent more time queuing outside immigration offices than I care to remember, only then having to hop on last-minute flights when permits don't come through in time.

Security and stability are hard to come by when you live a life in the wild. But I don't, for one second, regret any of it.

When the doctor told me my lungs were full of blood clots, I wasn't scared by the seriousness of my illness, I was distraught that it threatened my chance to get back to the bush. In that moment, the fear of having to continue living an ordinary life was much greater than the fear of dying. I hang on to that notion whenever I feel like the drama of life in the wild is getting overwhelming. Extreme highs and lows are part of life in the bush and, for me, riding those is better than living a life in monochrome.

I am older and wiser now though. I take less risks to get the close encounters, I have had enough misadventures to last me a lifetime. It is still about taking personal risks though - stepping outside my comfort zone, pushing my boundaries, to see what I am capable of. This is where the thrills come from.

It is these risks I have taken and the experiences I have had as a result, both good and bad, that have made me the person I am today. I have a greater sense of freedom now than I have ever had before. Whether that has come with age, or the reality-check that life can be cut short, I can't be sure. But the insecurities I used to suffer, about my abilities and my place in the world, are gone. I can be whoever I choose to be.

And, I choose to be a *Girl of the Wild*.

*"Wild girl with wild hair.
I see you and I know what you are up to.
You want the world and everything in it
and there is nothing anyone could do to stop you.
Just remember a tamed woman
will never leave her mark on the world.
Stay wild."*

- Robert M. Drake[15]